BLACK AMERICANS AND THEIR CONTRIBUTIONS TOWARD UNION VICTORY IN THE AMERICAN CIVIL WAR, 1861-1865

Joe H. Mays

UNIVERSITY
PRESS OF
AMERICA

LANHAM • NEW YORK • LONDON

Copyright © 1984 by

University Press of America,™ Inc.

4720 Boston Way
Lanham, MD 20706

3 Henrietta Street
London WC2E 8LU England

Library of Congress Cataloging in Publication Data

Mays, Joe H., 1939–
  Black Americans and their contributions toward Union
victory in the American Civil War, 1861–1865.

    Bibliography: p.
    Includes index.
    1. United States–History–Civil War, 1861–1865–
Participation, Afro-American. 2. United States. Army–
Afro-Americans–History–19th century. 1. Title.
E540.N3M23   1983   973.7'415   83–14727
ISBN 0–8191–3504–6 (alk. paper)
ISBN 0–8191–3505–4 (pbk. : alk. paper))

TO MY LOVING FAMILY

Dad
Jackie, Tony, Sheila, Alesha
Raymond, Louise, Bernice, Beatrice, James
Bessie, Katherine, Bennie, Eddie
Virginia

ACKNOWLEDGEMENTS

A book of this kind usually involves the work of more than one person. Many persons cooperated and offered their advice in helping me conduct this study. I would like to express my sincere gratitude to the following professors at Middle Tennessee State University: Dr. Thelma Jennings, Dr. Fred P. Colvin, Dr. Frederick S. Rolater, and Dr. Wallace R. Maples.

Special thanks are due the personnel of the Jackson State Community College Library, especially the reference librarian Scott R. Cohen. I am also grateful to these library staffs: Lambuth College and Freed Hardeman College for the use of their Official Records of the Union and Confederate Armies and Navies, the University of Tennessee at Martin, and Middle Tennessee State University. Above all, I would like to thank the library staffs at Lane College and Fisk University for their help and the use of their Black Heritage special collection section. They went beyond the call of duty many times in allowing me to use the special collection section after closing hours.

Finally, a special debt of gratitude is owed to Dr. Don E. Chevalia, Chairman of the Social Studies Division at Jackson State Community College, who helped me secure a leave of absence and a grant-in-aid. I am also indebted to Dr. Robert Harrell, Dean of Instruction, and Dr. Walter Nelms, President of Jackson State Community College, for their help and support. Special acknowledgement is also due Dr. Currie P. Boyd, a colleague, and Ms. Betty L. Curry, a special friend, for sharing in the frustrations and joys which transpired during the time to bring this study to a successful conclusion.

CONTENTS

INTRODUCTION

American history textbooks often fail to note the contributions black Americans have made toward the development to today's society, particularly their efforts toward Union victory in the Civil War. The belief still persists among many laymen, students, and some historians that the blacks were passive, docile, uncomprehending recipients of freedom in 1865.

American blacks were both symbols and participants in the war. They were not merely passive recipients of the benefits conferred upon them by the war, but were active on the battlefields, behind the lines, and on the home front. Approximately 520,000 blacks came within Union lines during the war. Most of them went to work as laborers, spies, scouts, guides, and servants, but more than 200,000 of them fought in the Union army and navy.

Black civilians made some noteworthy contributions to the war effort. Many black women worked in hospitals and camps, raised money for the families of the men at the front, and worked with convalescent soldiers. Black orators and writers were leaders in the struggle for emancipation and equal rights. They also worked to bring education, suffrage, and land to southern freedmen.

American blacks were crucial to the whole Union war effort. Not only did black soldiers, as well as other blacks, help the Union win the war, but they convinced many northern people that they deserved to be treated as equals. During their service in the Civil War, black soldiers participated in at least thirty-nine major battles and four hundred ten major engagements. They constituted twelve percent of the entire Federal armies and seventeen received the Congressional Medal of Honor, America's highest military honor.

Black Americans had fought in nearly every American war before the outbreak of the Civil War. They had fought in the colonial wars, in the Revolution, and in the War of 1812. Before the American Civil War, however, black Americans were not an official part of the regular military forces of the United States. They served in times of war, but after the crisis reverted to their previous status, slaves or free blacks. During the Civil War

American blacks permanently won the right to bear arms. Ever since then they have served in the regular army and in the militia of some of the states during peacetime.

The Civil War resulted in a revolution in the status of blacks, North as well as South. It brought freedom, citizenship, and eventually equal civil and political rights (in theory at least) to all American blacks. Thousands of freedmen received the rudiments of education. Time revealed that the revolution in the status of blacks was not as complete as it appeared, but in 1865 blacks could look backward on four years of startling and rapid change and could look forward hopefully to acceptance as equals in American life.

I have used many textbooks during my nineteen years of teaching experience on the secondary and college levels and have observed that a very brief coverage, if any at all, has been given to blacks and their contributions to the Union war effort. As one of the first blacks to teach in a predominantly white high school (Dyersburg High in 1965) in Tennessee and the first black instructor at Jackson State Community College in 1968, I have observed that both black and white students know little about the roles blacks played in the Civil War. They are also unaware of the available sources on the subject.

This book is important because it will provide resource materials that can be used in the reading and teaching of American history. Hopefully all students (black and white) will, therefore, have a more accurate description of the American Civil War. Moreover, an increasing number of white Americans have become aware that their lack of knowledge about the role of their black countrymen in the making of America has diminished their understanding of the past and their grasp on the social realities of the present.

When history books do not mention the many contributions that black Americans made toward Union victory, a significant omission has resulted. All Americans should realize or at least have an opportunity to learn that black Americans have been more than insignificant figures on the outskirts of American life, prominent only in athletics and entertainment. Often the positive contributions of black Americans have escaped the eye of the historian and have not been included in his work. It is, therefore, the purpose of this book (1) to develop a resource unit on the contributions of black Americans toward Union victory in the American Civil War, 1861-1865; and (2) to provide the laymen, students and instructors with a comprehensive bibliography for further study on the subject.

The validity of this book rests upon the following assumptions·

1.   Although many American history textbooks have recently been revised to correct their almost total neglect of the contributions of black Americans toward the total Union war effort, the result in most cases is unsatisfactory.

2.   Students of both races need to know the truth about America's past: therefore, the contribution of black Americans to the American culture must not be overlooked.

3.   Many American history teachers in high school and college survey courses give inadequate coverage to the numerous black contributions to the total Union war effort.

4.   An important goal of education is to study the contributions of all Americans and history should be taught with this in mind.

This study involved a thorough investigation of the secondary books about black Americans and their contributions during the American Civil War. In addition, The Journal of Negro History and other historical quarterlies were explored for articles. Doctoral dissertations and master's theses with titles related to this study were surveyed. Primary sources were also researched. These included the official records of the United States Government for both the armies and navies. Other contemporary source material was also investigated.

A number of writers have written in recent years on the role of black Americans during the American Civil War. A few of the most relevant works are: John Hope Franklin in From Slavery to Freedom (Chapter XVI), William L. Katz in Eyewitness: The Negro in American History (Chapter IX), James M. McPherson in The Negro's Civil War, Dudley T. Cornish in The Sable Arm, and Benjamin Quarles in The Negro in the Civil War. These noted writers agree that the prejudice against black soldiers after they were permitted to fight in the war made their circumstances much harder than those of the whites. Black soldiers received less pay than whites, were ineligible until near the end of the war to become officers, and were not treated as prisoners of war when captured. Yet many blacks realized the importance of remaining in the Union army. Not only would black troops help shorten the war and bring about the freedom of the slaves, but their participation would be their passport to citizenship. An important aspect of black involvement is the fact that most of the black soldiers came from the South and were former slaves. According to John Hope Franklin, 93,000 black troops were recruited from the seceded states; 40,000 came from the border slave states which remained in the Union; and 52,000 came from the free states. These figures should modify the view held by many historians about the loyalty of slaves during the war.

Blacks saw the coming of civil war in 1861 as the dawn of their day of freedom. After blacks were permitted to enlist as soldiers in the Union army and navy, they served in practically all major campaigns and battles. President Lincoln and many other persons in high places praised their bravery and devotion, and testified to the great importance of their contribution to the cause of victory.

All people need a sense of their past in order to live fully in the present. Human beings need to know where they have been if they are to know where they are and where they are going. Black Americans have been robbed of many things; among the most important has been their own history. As a teacher of American history, it seems to me that it is impossible to comprehend "American history" without some knowledge of the many contributions made to our culture by black Americans. It is my hope that this book will help students, teachers, and laymen (black and white) to have a more accurate description of the American Civil War.

CHAPTER I

FROM CONTRABAND TO SOLDIERS

Shortly after the fall of Fort Sumter on 15 April 1861, President Lincoln issued a call for 75,000 three-month volunteers and received an overwhelming response. The attack on Fort Sumter angered and almost united a divided North. On the day of the fort's surrender, the regular army numbered only 16,367 officers and men. Many black Americans answered President Lincoln's call for volunteers to suppress the rebellion but were turned away. Despite the fact that black soldiers had fought with distinction in the Revolution and in the War of 1812, state constitutions barred blacks from serving in state militias and no blacks were in the regular army at this time.[1]

Blacks throughout the North insisted that they should be permitted to enlist in the Union army. Frederick Douglass and other abolitionists, both black and white, urged blacks in northern cities to form militia companies. Within thirty-six hours of President Lincoln's first call for troops, a group of Boston blacks met and resolved to organize militia units. In subsequent weeks they sent several petitions to the state legislature pleading for the repeal of the discriminatory laws.[2]

Douglass believed the war presented an opportunity for blacks to fight in what he regarded as a crusade for liberty. He saw the end of slavery in the conflict. Because he conceived it as a war of emancipation, Douglass was anxious that blacks strike a blow. Two ideas thus took possession of Douglass from the moment the war started: free the slaves as a war measure and recruit the blacks into the Union army. In editorials, speeches, letters, and interviews, he stressed again and again this policy without compromise. Throughout the North, Douglass urged enlistment. He also argued that it was better to die free than to live as slaves. Douglass further believed that, if the blacks demonstrated their patriotism, manhood, and courage on the battlefields of the Union, the nation would be morally obligated to grant them citizenship and equal rights.[3]

Many local black leaders also took the initiative in recruiting black soldiers. When these leaders (often self-designated) had rounded up a sufficient number of volunteers, they would offer the

1

volunteers to the governor for enrollment in the state militia. In the early stages of the war much, therefore, depended upon community initiative. In Providence, Rhode Island, Samuel Dorrer organized a company of blacks, but the governor refused their services. The soldiers decided, however, to continue drilling in anticipation of later active service, but police officials told them that their drilling exercises were "disorderly gatherings" and would therefore be broken up. A group of black men began drilling in New York City in anticipation of a possible call to active service, but they were promptly told by the chief of police that they must cease their activities.[4]

In Cleveland, Washington, Detroit, Philadelphia, and many other cities throughout the North, blacks were told that "this is a white man's war" and their services as soldiers were promptly refused. In April 1861, Secretary of War Simon Cameron informed 300 black volunteers, who offered their help to defend the capital city, that his department had no intention at the present time of calling any black soldiers into the service of the government.[5] Public opinion in 1861, except perhaps in a few of the New England states, was overwhelmingly opposed to allowing blacks in the militia or the army as soldiers. In the Midwest there were thousands of southern sympathizers. Border and midwestern states were ready to denounce the government for anything that could be construed as pro-black. The mere mention of a black service man made the President and many in Washington very nervous.[6] Popular sentiment in the North was reflected in the House of Representatives resolution of 22 July 1861, declaring that the war was being waged not for the overthrow of the established institutions of the southern states, but for the upholding of the Constitution and the preservation of the Union. Three days later the Senate adopted a similar resolution.[7]

There were several reasons why blacks were refused enlistment in the Union army at the beginning of the war. From the beginning, President Lincoln made clear that his central purpose was to preserve the Union. He assured North and South that he would not interfere with slavery. While abolitionists, both black and white, called for an end to slavery and the use of black soldiers, Lincoln was concerned with keeping the loyalty of the four slave border states that remained in the Union. He also believed that most northerners would not support a war to end slavery.[8]

Many northerners argued that the black man was innately inferior in mental capacity to the white man and would not, or could not, fight. This belief was one of the main arguments for slavery and it also imposed a powerful obstacle to the advancement of free blacks in the North as well as in the South. Defenders of this belief further reiterated that blacks were by nature shiftless, childlike, savage, and thus incapable of performing accepted modes of warfare. The specters of Nat Turner, Santo Domingo, and other slave insurrections were regarded as sufficient warnings of what might happen if armed black men were unleashed upon white slaveholding families. Even if black enlistment should later become desirable, few whites believed that black men possessed the necessary technical skills, intelligence, and courage to become effective soldiers.[9]

Some northerners warned that white soldiers would not fight alongside black soldiers because prejudice against them was so strong that whites would not enlist or would leave the service if compelled to fight with blacks. Many northerners also argued that very few blacks would enlist in the Union army and that the use of blacks would exasperate many northerners to the extent that their enlistment would do more harm than good. With patriotic whites rallying to the President's call for volunteers, there seemed little reason to doubt that the rebellion would be easily and speedily crushed. Thus, there was no need for black soldiers.[10]

Abolitionists and other humanitarians worked tirelessly and unsuccessfully to combat these arguments. They argued from the pulpit, platform, and press that a hostile environment, not innate inferiority, had created the servile, comic creature that was the American concept of blacks in 1861. The abolitionists affirmed that, if this environment were changed by the abolition of slavery, the employment of black soldiers, and an end to racial discrimination, the blacks would prove themselves constructive, capable, and creative members of society.[11]

The exploits of black soldiers during the Revolution and the War of 1812 were brought to light by the abolitionists. They quoted Andrew Jackson's praise of the New Orleans blacks who helped defeat the British in 1815. Frederick Douglass sarcastically noted that black men were not considered good enough to fight under George McClellan, but they were good enough to fight under George Washington. He also stated that blacks were good enough to help win American independence, but they were not good enough to help preserve that independence against treason and rebellion. Douglass further pointed out that the Confederate army was employing blacks as nurses, cooks, servants, and laborers. As laborers in the Confederate army and behind the lines, the blacks relieved more whites to take up arms against the Union.[12]

Abolitionists also pointed to Toussaint L'Ouverture, the Haitian liberator who led his people out of slavery and defeated the armies of Napoleon when the French tried to re-enslave the Caribbean island. Black soldiers had proved their courage and ability in the American Revolution, the War of 1812, and Haiti, and would prove again in the Civil War that they make good soldiers if given the chance. Abolitionists further argued that black units would strengthen the Union army and sap the Confederacy of its manpower potentials. Black soldiers would give added meaning to American democracy. Military service would both prepare and justify blacks for full admittance into American society.[13]

The northern black man's eagerness to strike a blow, even though he was denied the wearing of the blue, was vividly illustrated by his service in other capacities. Some joined the navy, as the navy had never kept free blacks from enlisting. Others, determined to serve in the army, went as waiters, cooks, teamsters, and laborers. Many of the Providence blacks in the rejected company attached themselves as servants to Rhode Island regiments and batteries.[14]

In the South during the early years of the war, the slave owners saw the protection of slavery largely in terms of controlling slave behavior. Since slaves themselves had always been considered the chief threat to the institution, it was natural that the thinking of the slave owners began there. Masters constructed a strategy of defense based on the prewar precedent of isolation. Their aim was to keep the slaves in and abolitionist ideas out of the South. If dangerous notions were kept out of the slave quarters and the slaves kept on the plantations, slavery would be secure. Thus, southerners began to set up methods of isolating the slaves as well as preventing uprisings and thwarting escapes. Under the Confederate constitution the central government was required to recognize

4

and protect slavery. State governors were required to return runaways who fled within their borders, and each state pledged to the citizens of other states the right to claim and transport their slave property. The free blacks were watched closely and state laws were passed for the dual purpose of keeping down the number of free blacks and reducing their contacts with the slaves. To prevent an increase in the free black population, some states prevented slave manumissions except by legislative action. All southern states now prevented free blacks from hiring or owning slaves to further reduce contacts between the two groups. They were also prevented from meeting or gathering with slaves.[15]

The most widely used method of directly controlling the slave population was that of policing. Each plantation had guards whose duty it was to patrol the roads after dark. These guards, employed by the planters, were recognized by the local and state authorities. The curfew and passport were measures used to keep the blacks off the streets and roads without permission. Slave passes off the plantations virtually ceased. To help control the slaves, many owners permitted more privileges and recreation (annual barbecue, group singing, Saturday night dances, possum hunts, weddings, etc.) on the plantations as means of winning their loyalty. The religious training of the slaves emphasized the importance of the slaves' loyalty and obedience to their masters.[16]

Control through fear was more widely practiced than through kindness. Masters told their slaves that the Union soldiers had no mercy for them. Captured blacks would be put in the front line of battle to be killed. Or they might be harnessed and used as horses. Some northerners would even sell captured blacks to Cuba. Another form of slave control was impressment. Six states authorized their governors to employ slaves for non-combatant military service. Slave masters received fifty cents a day for each slave's service. Removal was another method of controlling the slaves. When the Union soldiers began their invasion of the South, the exposed areas of the plantations were abandoned. The plantation owners and their slaves would abandon their homes and move to a special constructed safe area near the interior of the plantation. Many planters also withdrew their slaves from the towns. Shortly after the war started, southern roads were swarming with blacks being transferred to safer spots. This movement, "running the blacks," as it was called, became a familiar spectacle.[17]

The various methods of controlling the blacks could not be fully effective without the cooperation of the blacks themselves. Whether the slaves would remain loyal and obedient to their mistresses became a major topic of discussion throughout the South as the men went off to battle. Southerners, with great relief, began to boast of slave loyalty when it became apparent that there would be no general large-scale uprisings. Local patriotism, freedom after the war, fear, and loyalty were some of the motivating factors that at first kept most blacks working peacefully on the plantations. To many blacks in the South, however, the war went hand in hand with freedom. The desire of the slaves for freedom was evidenced by the way in which they received the Union troops. The Union soldiers were almost always cheerfully welcomed by the blacks in the invaded areas.[18]

The desire for freedom was so strong in thousands of slaves that they decided not to wait for the coming of the Union soldiers or the end of the war. Since freedom might be too long in coming, they set out to find freedom themselves. Deserting slaves began to enter Union lines seeking freedom shortly after the war started. The United States government had no clear policy regarding the deserting slaves. President Lincoln had announced to the army that the real object of its service was "to restore the seceding state" to their constitutional relation to the Union. The slavery question, therefore, had no place in the early military policy of the Union army. Slaves as property were recognized and sustained by the Constitution.[19]

Union policy toward the slaves slowly began to change. On 23 May 1861, three slaves, owned by Colonel Charles Mallory of Hampton, fled to Fortress Monroe, Virginia. Through interrogation of the three slaves, General Benjamin Butler, Union commander of the Department of Virginia, learned that the Confederates in Hampton had forced them and other slaves to construct Confederate defenses. John B. Cary, a major in the Confederate army, requested that General Butler surrender the three blacks to their owner under the Fugitive Slave Law. Butler refused to give them up. He argued that since these blacks were used to erect fortifications for the South they were contraband of war in the same sense as captured guns or ammunition.[20]

Benjamin Butler was no abolitionist, and his reasons for declaring the fugitives contraband of war were legal and practical rather than moral. Under the circumstances, General Butler thought that Union forces were justified in appropriating slave property for their own use. He was in need of labor; the slaves had been used against the United States by their owners and he believed he was empowered to impress this species of "property" into service for the United States. Butler further reasoned that, by virtue of the blacks' role in the Confederate construction program, he could classify the men as contraband goods and thus give them refuge at Fortress Monroe. He did not question the sanctity of slave property, only its use. General Butler may have been the first to use the word "contraband" as applied to human beings. The word was speedily adopted by many people. It was later used in all official communications; the North was reluctant about calling the runaways free men, but it had no objections to calling them contrabands.[21]

The news of General Butler's contraband decision quickly became known to the slaves in the vicinity. Two days after Butler denied Major Cary's request, eight more blacks arrived and fifty-nine joined them the following day. Fearing family separation, many blacks arrived with entire families. By July, scarcely two months after the first three fugitives arrived at Fortress Monroe, the number of refugees in the area had reached six hundred. Soon these fugitives were performing most of the various services needed around the army camp. They were used as teamsters, cooks, officers' servants, and laborers. The President's cabinet met and discussed the question of Butler's contraband policy. Although Lincoln believed the problem required further thought, he allowed the Secretary of War to approve Butler's action.[22]

Blacks continued to come into Union lines at Fortress Monroe during the summer of 1861. Veteran abolitionist Lewis Tappan, a leading figure in the American Missionary Association, suggested directly to Butler that the contrabands might be removed to the North. In the North the refugees could find employment on the farms and in the workshops of loyal northern citizens. Butler decided to keep them in Virginia rather than relocate them in the North. To send large numbers of agricultural laborers North, where their labor was not wanted, seemed unwise to him. He maintained that the blacks could be better and more economically cared for in the South where the climate was warm and where there was considerable abandoned property to accommodate them. Furthermore, he saw in the blacks a potential agricultural and labor force.[23]

For the fugitives, Fortress Monroe offered protection. Butler's policy had the character of an open invitation for the slaves. Although the war itself was barely underway, the fortress became the first center of refuge for the slaves. Reconstruction, as far as blacks were concerned, had begun. According to Sister Elizabeth Allen, Butler's decision liberated thousands of black people eighteen months before Lincoln's Emancipation Proclamation.[24]

Butler had the responsibility of providing for the contrabands. In July 1861 he began using large numbers of contrabands to construct breastworks around the town of Hampton. He assigned Edward L. Pierce as superintendent of contraband labor, because of his antislavery background and his administrative ability. Pierce believed that the blacks would work better by kind treatment than by being whipped and driven. He wanted to prove that blacks would work as free men. Under his direction, the blacks worked nine hours a day, the same as white laborers, and received the same rations as the soldiers. Their workday began at dawn to avoid the hottest portion of the afternoon. Pierce worked with the contrabands only a short time before he was reassigned as superintendent of confiscated cotton plantations in the South Carolina Sea Islands. According to Pierce, his program for the contrabands at Fortress Monroe was a success. In mid-August 1861 Butler was also transferred from Virginia. He was later assigned to the Department of the Gulf to prepare for capturing New Orleans. The abolitionists praised Butler for his contraband decision at Fortress Monroe. Before his transfer, however, he admitted that the growing number of contrabands under his control had become a major problem.[25]

By land and by sea, the fugitives were resourceful in carrying out their escapes. Since tidewater Virginia, the area of earliest Union control, was a network of streams, many of the first blacks made their way to freedom by water. Many simply put their possessions on fishing boats and under cover of darkness pushed down the river. Unable to find boats, some determined blacks made canoes. Some of these canoes were simply hollowed logs large enough for one person. In order to prevent bloodhounds from picking up their trail, the fugitives applied turpentine to their shoes and feet. Onions were also used to destroy scent. The practice of forging passes as officers' servants was often used by the few blacks who were literate.[26]

The number of blacks coming into the Union lines inevitably mounted as the Union armies pushed farther into Confederate heartland. The slaves deserted despite the heavy risks. Many were captured and some killed by the Confederate patrol units and pickets. Those who escaped by sea ran the danger of having the boats swamped by water or upset by wind. According to Benjamin Quarles, this movement by individuals, by families, and groups was unparalleled in American history for daring, sacrifice, and heroism. These fugitives became one of the most insistent problems of the Lincoln administration, as Butler's contraband policy did not apply to slaves of loyal owners or to women and children.[27]

Politically, the fugitive issue was very sensitive. Neither the President nor the War Department took a firm position and every commander, lacking clear instructions, acted as he chose. In the opening months of the war before northern manpower losses became heavy and before the large-scale invasion of the South, a majority of the generals was cool toward the runaways. Returning the runaways to their masters was a common practice and one that was supported by the administration. Confederates also came to some northern camps under a flag of truce and seized their runaways.[28]

The indiscriminate return of fugitive slaves to their masters aroused public sentiment in the North that almost amounted to indignation. Abolitionists, such as Henry W. Beecher, William Lloyd Garrison, Wendell Phillips, and Frederick Douglass, urged the President to free and employ the slaves. Phillips declared there could be no peace until slavery was abolished. The abolitionists further stated that the three and a half million slaves in the eleven Confederate states constituted nearly forty percent of their population and a majority of their labor force. After the Union defeat at Bull Run in July 1861, attributed in part to the Confederate military defenses constructed by slaves, Congress began to pressure the President. This defeat also ended the delusion of a short war and diminished northern enlistment enthusiasm. In July 1861, the House passed a resolution declaring that it was not the duty of Union soldiers to capture and return fugitives. A few weeks later, on 6 August, Congress passed the first Confiscation Act which declared that all slaves whose masters had permitted them to be used in the military or naval service of the Confederacy were forfeited.[29]

The first Confiscation Act did not disturb the legal status of slaves. By the terms of this act, all property (including slaves) used to aid the Confederacy was subject to confiscation. Southern blacks were not declared free, but were simply confiscated from their owners. This act provided a legal sanction for Butler's policy at Fortress Monroe. Federal officers might confiscate the slaves of disloyal and rebellious persons, but the status of fugitives from loyal masters remained uncertain. This action of Congress, however, strengthened those few antislavery Union officers who from the beginning were in favor of freeing the slaves. One antislavery commander whose action drew national attention during this time was John C. Fremont. In command of the Department of the West, he declared martial law in Missouri on 30 August 1861. Under his martial law, the property, real and personal, of all persons in the state of Missouri who had taken up arms against the United States and who could be proven to have cooperated with the enemies was to be confiscated for the public use and their slaves freed.[30]

There was jubilation in antislavery circles. Abolitionists hoped Fremont's bold action would inspire other generals to take similar action and perhaps persuade the President to change his position. President Lincoln did not take the abolitionist viewpoint. He sent a message informing Fremont that his actions would alarm the Union's southern friends and requested that he modify his proclamation to conform to the first Confiscation Act. General Fremont declined to do this and accordingly, on 11 September, the President modified that portion of the proclamation. Fremont was subsequently removed and the task of subduing rebels and freeing blacks was suspended.[31]

Fremont was replaced by General Henry W. Hallock, who excluded fleeing slaves from his lines. General George McClellan, an avowed foe of emancipation of blacks, was promoted to general-in-chief in November 1861. Blacks in general and white abolitionists became furious with the President. When Lincoln ignored the whole issue of black freedom in his message to Congress a month later, their frustrations increased.[32]

Militant blacks, such as Frederick Douglass, were further disturbed by one of the immediate consequences of the President's policy. It stimulated already widespread black cynicism about the war, and thus inhibited the struggle for black participation. Although the Confiscation Act on 6 August 1861 warranted and justified the employment of fugitive slaves in a military capacity, no legislation had been passed to enroll the blacks as soldiers. Only the use of fugitive slaves of persons in actual rebellion against the United States was contemplated to this point. No attention was paid to the free blacks of the northern states who could supply 25,000 able-bodied, patriotic soldiers.[33]

During the latter part of 1861, apparently Lincoln had no intention of doing anything against slavery. The large number of blacks coming into Union lines continued to create problems. The increasing black population, particularly of women and children, far exceeded the number the army could profitably employ. General John E. Wool, Butler's successor at Fortress Monroe, found the problem of employing the able-bodied, while supporting the dependent blacks, a pressing one. He requested instructions from Secretary of War Simon Cameron concerning this problem. Cameron suggested that he send all able-bodied blacks, along with their families, to General George McClellan at Washington to work on the capital's defenses. Wool's essential problem, however, was with the large population of women and children.[34]

The total contraband population at Fortress Monroe by March 1862 had grown to approximately 1,500 and the number of women and children was about 850. Though most of the women and children were not employed, some were used as cooks and servants. In an attempt to justify army care of destitute blacks, Wool adopted a wage system. He ordered all officers and soldiers who had black servants to pay monthly wages of at least eight dollars for men and four for women. The wages went to the quartermaster who managed the funds for the benefit of the destitute blacks, after deductions for the cost of clothing. Those blacks actually employed seldom received pay; their earnings were simply applied to the care of the non-laboring population. However, at the discretion of the chief of each department exceptionally diligent laborers might receive fifty cents to two dollars pay directly to them each month.[35]

By early 1862, it had become clear that a permanent program for the care and employment of arriving blacks had to be established. Blacks were coming into Union lines by the thousands. General Ulysses S. Grant found it necessary to

appoint John Eaton to take charge of all fugitives in his West
Tennessee area. A special camp was set up for blacks at Grand
Junction, Tennessee, where Eaton supervised the hiring of these
fugitives and leasing abandoned land to whites who hired them.
He made sure that they were paid for their work. In Louisiana,
General Butler leased blacks to loyal planters who paid ten
dollars monthly for each.[36]

A federal policy for relief of freedmen developed so slowly
that private persons, both black and white, began to organize
throughout northern cities for the express purpose of rendering
more effective aid to the blacks in the South. The National
Freedmen's Relief Association was organized in New York on 22
February 1862. Soon thereafter the Contraband Relief Association
in Cincinnati, the Friends Association for the Relief of Colored
Freedmen in Philadelphia, and the Northwestern Freedmen's Aid
Commission of Chicago were organized. Religious organizations,
led by the American Missionary Association, joined in the relief
of the blacks. Clothing and food were solicited, collections
were made, and representatives were sent South to minister to
the needs of the ex-slaves. This transition period for the blacks
was extremely difficult. Because of the confused and changing
federal policy, there was much suffering and death among the
blacks in these contraband camps.[37]

In an attempt to reduce the confusion in the employment and
relief of the fugitives, Secretary of War Edwin Stanton in late
April 1862 directed General Rufus Saxton, commander of the
Department of the South, to take full charge of abandoned
plantations and the blacks. Stanton authorized Saxton to make
whatever rules and regulations necessary for the successful
cultivation of the land and the organization of laborers. Stanton,
who had replaced Simon Cameron as Secretary of War in January
1862, believed that the Confederacy was a conspiracy of traitors
and that total war was necessary to destroy it. Aid, emancipation,
and the military use of the blacks became weapons of war for him.
Stanton could not sympathize with Lincoln's cautious approach to
these problems. Thus, he turned to the radical leaders in
Congress for support in an attempt to wage total war against the
South and in dealing with the refugees. Cordial relations,
therefore, prevailed between Stanton and the radical leaders in
Congress which lasted throughout the war and reconstruction years.

Stanton pressed for the abolition and arming of the slaves in cabinet meetings with the President throughout 1862.[38]

General Saxton issued an order in the winter of 1862 for a general plan to be followed everywhere in his department concerning the problems of the fugitives and abandoned lands. Southern abandoned lands would be divided into two areas and a superintendent appointed to supervise each area. Ex-slaves would work the land with each family allotted two acres for each working hand. All black families would be required to raise a certain amount of cotton for government use and to plant corn and potatoes for their own use. From these plots blacks were expected to provide their own subsistence. Wages were paid for the planting, hoeing, and picking of the government's cotton. The tools would be furnished by the government. The superintendent also had the responsibility of protecting those blacks in his area who hired themselves out to white employers and further seeing that they had the necessities of life.[39]

General Saxton's plan did not work very well. One difficulty was the small amount of land available for use by the blacks. The government was selling much of the land to private persons; and frequently these new owners had little interest in the plight of the blacks. Some of the appointed superintendents showed little interest in the problems of the blacks. Furthermore, the Treasury Department contested the right of the War Department to administer the affairs of the blacks. Although the Secretary of War desired the Treasury to control all confiscated property, except that used by the military, officers in the field were of the opinion that they could best handle everything.[40]

One of the most important and highly publicized attempts to make the contrabands self-supporting took place at Port Royal, South Carolina. In November 1861 Union forces captured Port Royal Island and the adjacent South Carolina Sea Islands fifty miles southwest of Charleston. The entire white population fled the island as the Union forces advanced. The federal troops occupied Beaufort with more than 60,000 acres of arable land and about 10,000 slaves. The situation at Port Royal demanded immediate action and extensive organization. Northern blacks and white abolitionists took a special interest in Port Royal. Because of their physical and cultural isolation from the mainland, the slaves on these islands were among the most backward in the entire South. The blacks and white abolitionists, therefore,

13

reasoned that, if these slaves proved themselves capable of a productive and useful life in freedom, anti-emancipation arguments based on the alleged innate inferiority of the blacks would be seriously hampered.[41]

Secretary of the Treasury Salmon P. Chase also took an immediate interest in Port Royal. Chase selected his friend and associate, Edward L. Pierce (formerly Butler's superintendent of contrabands at Fortress Monroe), to go to the Sea Islands and look into the contraband situation. After spending nearly a month in Port Royal, Pierce devised a plan to make the blacks self-supporting and the cotton plantations profitable to the federal government. Under Pierce's plan, the territory was divided into districts and each district had a superintendent and a teacher. Freedmen's aid societies provided clothes, school supplies, teachers, missionaries, nurses, and medical supplies. Under Pierce's management the contrabands grew corn, potatoes, sorghum for molasses, and cotton. The superintendents rationed supplies and the teachers instructed them to read and write.[42]

Most participants and observers of the "Port Royal Experiment" concluded that it was a success. After a year, thirty schools had been established on the Sea Islands and an average of 2,000 pupils reported daily for instruction. Crop production, except cotton, increased tremendously. Proponents further argued that the results of Port Royal indicated that with assistance, guidance, and a fair chance the slaves could be converted to free laborers without violent social dislocation.[43]

The issue of freeing the slaves continued to plague the administration. Lincoln believed slavery was wrong; however, he held that the Presidency did not confer on him the right to act upon his feelings and beliefs. As a believer in democracy, he was guided by public opinion and hence he tended to delay action until the people had voiced their views. Lincoln believed that the best solution to the slavery problem was gradual compensated emancipation. Under this plan the slave masters would be paid out of the national treasury for the loss of their slaves. He thought that if he could get one border state to take this step the others would follow. Delaware was selected because it had less than two thousand slaves. Lincoln estimated the government could pay four hundred dollars each for Delaware's slaves and it would cost less than the war cost for a day. In November 1861 he submitted his proposal privately to a friend of the Delaware legislature for introduction. The proposal received a stormy reception in the state legislature. The criticism was so vigorous that the bill was withdrawn before it was formally introduced.[44]

The President was not deterred by the rejection of his proposal in Delaware. On 6 March 1862, President Lincoln sent a message to Congress recommending passage of a joint resolution offering federal compensation to any state that adopted a plan of gradual abolition of slavery. His proposal was widely discussed and received generally favorable comments in the press. On 10 April, Congress by joint resolution passed the proposal exactly as Lincoln had worded it in his message. The border states rejected the proposal in their respective legislatures. Abolitionists, both black and white, nevertheless welcomed the proposal as a sign of a major shift in the administration's policy toward slavery.[45]

The sharp setback to compensated emancipation of the slaves resulted in a second plan by the President--colonization outside the country. Many conservatives remained unconvinced that large numbers of freed slaves could remain in the United States without causing social upheaval. They opposed emancipation except upon the condition of colonization. They further believed that free blacks represented a dangerous social class which could never be effectively integrated into the social fabric. In 1861-62 there was widespread support among conservative Republicans and Democrats for the colonization abroad of blacks emancipated by the war. Lincoln believed that deportation would simultaneously achieve two ends: get rid of slavery and get rid of the blacks. The idea of removing the blacks was by no means original with Lincoln. It had been discussed and debated for years as a means of ridding the nation of its slavery and race problems.[46]

For more than forty years the American Colonization Society and its state auxiliaries had sought to solve the race problem by colonizing free blacks in Africa. Opposed by most blacks, white abolitionists, and moderates, this project overall was a failure. With the war and the flight of fugitives to Union lines, however, colonization of blacks gained widespread support. Some suggested voluntary and others compulsory colonization. Many leading men in the early part of the Civil War offered colonization as the magic solution to the black problem. It was the consensus of the supporters of colonization that blacks and whites could never live together peacefully as equals. Colonization, therefore, was the only possible solution to the slavery and racial problems. Some northern blacks, embittered by their second-class citizen status, favored colonization. These blacks wanted to establish a prosperous black republic that would disprove the myth of the black man's inability to govern himself and, at the same time, escape white prejudice. The opponents of colonization argued that most blacks had no desire to leave the United States, their homeland, and denounced the colonization schemes.[47]

On 14 August 1862, President Lincoln met with an invited committee of blacks at the White House to discuss the issue of colonization. He urged them to consider the idea of colonization. He stated that slavery was the greatest wrong inflicted on any people, but even if the institution were abolished racial differences and prejudices would remain. Lincoln further stated that blacks had little chance for equality in the United States and that there was an unwillingness on the part of many whites for free blacks to remain in the country. It would therefore be better for the two races to be separated. Lincoln implored the black delegation to recruit several hundred fellow blacks for a pilot colonization project to demonstrate its feasibility as a solution to the race problem.[48]

Most northern blacks and white abolitionists condemned the President's proposal. Nevertheless, Lincoln gave his support to several unsuccessful colonization schemes during the war. He had come to the conclusion that the two races could not live harmoniously together as equals. Lincoln and other proponents of colonization thought that most blacks would prefer to emigrate rather than remain in America as second-class citizens. He, therefore, persuaded Congress during its 1861-62 session to appropriate $600,000 to help finance voluntary emigration of blacks to Liberia and Haiti. In 1862 the President signed a contract with Bernard Knock, a colonization promoter, for the colonization of 500 freed slaves on the Ile A 'Vache, a small island off the southern coast of Haiti. This emigration experiment to Ile A 'Vache, as well as other colonization attempts, was a disastrous failure. After getting the money, Knock failed to provide the blacks with adequate housing. Many blacks died from smallpox and starvation. Lincoln finally admitted failure and sent a ship to bring the survivors back to the United States in February 1864.[49]

Lincoln's colonization schemes failed partly because the status of blacks had begun to change as a result of the war. There was a great deal of antislavery activity in Washington in the spring of 1862. Congress passed a new article of war prohibiting army officers (on penalty of dismissal) from returning fugitive slaves who entered their lines. Legislation prohibiting slavery in all the territories of the United States and providing for the effactual suppression of the African slave trade was also enacted. Most dramatic of all was the passage in April of an act abolishing slavery in the District of Columbia, with compensation to the owners.[50]

A strong feeling was not manifested all over the North in favor of a vigorous war policy of freeing the slaves, and in many quarters the arming of blacks was regarded with favor. Many groups began to urge the President to emancipate the slaves and arm the blacks. As the North suffered more and more adversities on the battlefield, the demand for employing blacks as soldiers increased. With enlistments dwindling and manpower needs becoming more acute, the slaves of the enemy represented a source of strength both as military laborers and soldiers. Several Union generals urged Lincoln to free the slaves and arm the blacks. Moreover, the freeing of the slaves would strike a popular chord in England and on the Continent, undermining the Confederacy's efforts to win diplomatic recognition in the capitals of Europe.[51]

General David Hunter insisted on the use of blacks as soldiers. As commander of the Union forces occupying the islands off the coast of South Carolina, Georgia, and Florida, he proclaimed martial law in the Department of the South comprising all three states. He later declared all slaves in these states to be free and organized and armed the first black regiment composed of former slaves from these three states in April and May 1862. On 19 May, Lincoln declared, however, that neither General Hunter nor any other commander or person had been authorized by the United States government to make proclamations declaring the slaves of any state free. General Hunter was instructed to use the blacks as laborers and servants rather than soldiers.[52]

17

Despite the government's official opposition to black soldiers, several Union generals continued to organize black regiments during the summer of 1862. General James H. Lane of Kansas raised two black regiments composed of fugitive slaves from Missouri and free blacks from the North. Lane's black troops participated in several encounters against rebel forces in Kansas and Missouri, though they were not officially recognized by the War Department until early 1863. Free blacks in New Orleans, who had formed a Confederate regiment in 1861, offered their services to Union General Butler after the fall of the city in the spring of 1862. Butler refused the offer at first, but when he was threatened by a Confederate attack in August he gladly accepted the free blacks. General John W. Phelps, commander of Camp Parapet, a few miles west of New Orleans, organized five companies of former slaves. On 30 July 1862, he sent to Butler's headquarters requisitions for supplies for three black regiments which he proposed to raise for the defense of Camp Parapet. In reply to this request, Butler stated that the President alone had authority to employ blacks as soldiers.[53]

Meanwhile, northern public opinion began gradually to change toward arming the blacks. In the summer of 1862 Union forces suffered a series of military defeats. Mounting casualties, the returning wounded veterans, the alarming increase in desertions, and the growing difficulty in obtaining enlistments led to a reassessment of the military value of emancipation and black recruitment. On 17 July 1862, Congress passed a new confiscation act, the first direct legislation that sought the blacks' military assistance. This act empowered the President to accept blacks to perform war service for which they were competent. Although the President signed it, he was still opposed to the employment of blacks as soldiers.[54]

There was still a considerable amount of opposition in the North to the enlistment of black soldiers, but on 25 August 1862 the War Department, nevertheless, authorized General Rufus Saxton, military governor of the South Carolina Sea Islands, to raise five regiments of black troops on the islands with white men as officers. The First South Carolina Volunteers regiment was soon formed and Thomas W. Higginson was appointed its commander. Higginson was a Boston aristocrat, a Unitarian minister, a writer and lecturer, and a militant abolitionist. He was a captain in the Fifty-first Massachusetts Militia when he

received the letter from General Saxton which offered hi'
command of the first official black regiment with the rank ﹀
colonel. Most northern whites believed that black men,
especially ex-slaves, were to servile and cowardly to be good
soldiers. Higginson disagreed with this view and felt he had to
disprove this opinion. He was confident that blacks could be
trained to become good soldiers.[55]

Higginson was excited about commanding the first regiment of
black men officially mustered into the Union army. He fully
realized the importance of his undertaking. Higginson knew that
the eyes of the nation would be focused on this experiment, and
he wanted nothing to go wrong. He insisted that the white
officers of his regiment treat the black soldiers as men and he
inspired respect in his officers and confidence and self-respect
in his men. After two months of intensive drilling, Higginson
took his troops on several minor raids to capture supplies. His
soldiers fought well when they encountered Confederate soldiers.
Higginson stated in his first report to the Secretary of War that
no officer in his regiment doubted that the key to the successful
prosecution of the war lay in the unlimited employment of black
troops.[56]

At first most white soldiers grumbled at the prospect of
freed slaves serving in the same army. But by the spring of 1863
Higginson's soldiers had won a grudging, if not always generous,
respect from the white troops. While serving as commander of
the First South Carolina Volunteers, Higginson kept a journal in
which he recorded his observations and experiences. This
journal formed the basis of a book published in 1870 under the
title Army Life in a Black Regiment, one of the true classics of
the Civil War.[57]

Higginson's comments in his journal on the character of the
ex-slaves and their adaptability to military life are significant.
He stated that the freedmen were equal in courage and superior
in enthusiasm to white soldiers. Because their plantation
background had made them amenable to discipline, the blacks
took more readily to drill than whites. Higginson further stated
that they made better overall soldiers than whites, mainly
because of their knowledge of the countryside and their grim
comprehension that they were fighting for their freedom.[58]

The authorization to raise black regiments was of importance because blacks were now in the service of the United States by the War Department authority rather than by some enterprising general officer acting on his own initiative. This act signified a major turning point in the war policy of the Lincoln administration. Lincoln had made it clear less than three weeks earlier that he was not in favor of arming blacks as soldiers, but Secretary of War Stanton had now authorized that very thing. Lincoln permitted his secretary to issue this order mainly because of changing military events during that three-week period.[59]

In August 1862, the governor of Rhode Island also officially appealed to the black citizens of his state to enlist as soldiers. This was the first official call for black troops in the North. Less than three weeks later, on 22 August, General Butler, with headquarters in New Orleans, published his General Orders No. 63 calling on the free black militiamen of Louisiana to enroll in the volunteer forces of the Union.[60] Butler did not issue a general invitation to all black men of Louisiana; it specified only those free black men who had been enrolled in the Louisiana militia by the Confederate state government. He was not yet ready to arm slaves openly. Free blacks welcomed Butler's appeal and on 27 September 1862 the First Regiment Louisiana Native Guards, sanctioned by the War Department, was mustered into federal service. It was followed on 12 October by the Second Regiment and on 24 November by the Third Regiment.[61]

In the early days of September 1862 a sense of despondency settled heavily upon the northern people. General Pope's loss of the second Battle of Bull Run was a fearful blow. But on 17 September General George B. McClellan turned back General Robert E. Lee's invasion of Maryland at Sharpsburg. Seizing upon this as the victory for which he had waited, the President unexpectedly issued his preliminary Emancipation Proclamation five days later. It stipulated that, on 1 January 1863, all slaves in rebellious states would be declared forever free; loyal slave states and any rebellious states which returned to the Union before that time would be exempt from the terms of the edict. Lincoln also promised to present to Congress in December a plan for the gradual, compensated abolition of slavery in the loyal states. Limited as it was, the proclamation marked a strategic shift in the President's thinking about the military use of black men.[62]

In the weeks following 22 September, many people thought
Lincoln might retreat. There was strong conservative pressure
for modification or revocation. The Democrats made opposition
to emancipation one of their main issues in the 1862 congressional
elections, appealing to northern race prejudice and to the white
workingman's fear of low-wage competition from free blacks.
When the elections went against the Republicans, some of the
President's advisors blamed the preliminary proclamation and
urged him to recall it. [63]

Abolitionists were encouraged during this period by
Lincoln's ability to resist conservative pressure and by his
removal of the conservative General McClellan from command
of the Army of the Potomac on 7 November. But in his annual
message to Congress on 1 December, Lincoln dealt a sharp blow
to abolitionists' confidence. The President urged adoption of a
constitutional amendment granting compensation to any state
that undertook to abolish slavery by 1900. Slaves already free
would remain free, but all others would remain slaves until they
were gradually emancipated by the respective states or
individual owners. Abolitionists were astounded by this proposal.
The President's proposal was discussed in Congress, but no
such amendment was introduced. [64]

As the decisive New Year's Day drew near, blacks and white
abolitionists grew tense and anxious. Lincoln devoted more and
more time to the proclamation. On 29 December, he read his
proposed final document to the cabinet and received favorable
reaction. Lincoln carefully justified the proclamation by relying
on the powers vested in him as commander-in-chief of the
military of the United States in time of actual armed rebellion,
and by specifically calling the proclamation "a fit and necessary
war measure" to suppress insurrection. [65]

New Year's Day in 1863 was bright and sunny in Washington.
President Lincoln rose early and without special ceremony placed
his signature on the Emancipation Proclamation. He asked the
former slaves to sustain from violence and to labor faithfully.
He also invited them to join the armed forces. The impact of the
Proclamation on blacks was profound. Blacks regarded it as a
document of freedom, and they made no clear distinction between
the areas affected by the Proclamation and those not affected by
it. Frederick Douglass referred to the issuance of the

Proclamation as the greatest event of our nation's history, if not the greatest event of the century. The black grapevine in the South carried the news. As Union armies approached, slaves left the plantations, clinging to the soldiers despite ill-treatment, hunger, disease, and high death rate.[66]

Not until his final proclamation of 1 January 1863 did Lincoln publicly endorse the use of blacks as soldiers. Once committed to the revolutionary step of emancipation as a military measure, the Lincoln administration found it more and more impossible to reject the logic of permitting blacks to help secure their own freedom as soldiers. The administration became thoroughly committed to the use of black troops during the next several months after the Emancipation Proclamation.[67]

Within two weeks of the issuance of the Proclamation, Rhode Island was authorized to enlist blacks and shortly thereafter Governor John Andrew of Massachusetts received similar power. Andrew wanted to grant a few commissions to qualified blacks and give the opportunities for promotion, but Stanton and Lincoln feared the reaction of the northern people if black men became officers. All commissioned officers of black units were, therefore, white (less than a hundred blacks later became officers). Andrew wanted his first black regiment to be the grandest achievement of his governorship, and he took great care in selecting its officers. Recruiting proceeded slowly at first. Massachusetts' black population was too small to fill up a regiment. Andrew called on abolitionist George L. Stearns, a wealthy lead-pipe manufacturer and a leading advocate of black troops, to form a committee of prominent citizens to recruit soldiers for the Fifty-fourth Massachusetts Regiment from all over the North. The legislature appropriated funds for bounties and transportation of recruits to Massachusetts.[68]

Stearns hired several black leaders as recruiting agents, including Frederick Douglass, Martin Delany, William W. Brown, and John Mercer Langston. These men traveled throughout the North making speeches and urging blacks to join the army. Douglass was extremely active, and his own sons were the first recruits from New York. Blacks responded so readily that what was to become a historic regiment--the Fifty-fourth Massachusetts (the first official black regiment of the North)--was soon filled and another, the Fifty-fifth, was organized.[69]

Governor Andrew's success in raising two black regiments encouraged state troop quotas. In Philadelphia J. Miller McKim, a member of the Union League, started a movement within the League to enlist black troops from Pennsylvania. Within ten months, ten regiments of black troops from Pennsylvania and neighboring states were recruited and organized. With permission from Governor David Tod, John M. Langston of Ohio organized a regiment of black soldiers using his experience gained as a recruiting agent under Stearns.[70]

Action through the states, however, proved too slow to meet the manpower needs of an army suffering from high casualties, mounting desertions, and declining white enlistments. In March 1863, Adjutant General Lorenzo Thomas was sent to the Mississippi Valley with authority to raise black troops. By the end of the year he had organized twenty black regiments. The enterprise of recruiting and organizing black troops grew to such proportions that competent and appropriate machinery had to be constituted at Washington. General Orders No. 143, dated 22 May 1863, established the Bureau for Colored Troops with authority to supervise the organizing of black units and to examine candidates seeking commissions in them. This was a milestone in the history of blacks in the Civil War. For the remainder of the war, the organization of black regiments was on a uniform national basis whether those regiments were raised in northern states or in southern regions under Union control. Black soldiers were no longer fighting for a particular state or individual; they were fighting for the United States, the government that had promised them freedom. All black units were now called United States Colored Troops.[71]

The recruiting campaign for black soldiers in the North accelerated. Advertisements and dramatic plans for fund raising appeared in many newspapers. The emotionalism of wartime poured into the recruiting campaign. Despite discrimination against black soldiers, the pleas, speeches, circulars, pamphlets, posters, music, parades and rallies carried with them the theme of glory to be gained as a result of going to battle. War songs and poems were distributed for the black population to consume. The exploits of black soldiers during the Revolution and the War of 1812 were revealed in an attempt to provide a basis for the fighting tradition of the black man in American history.[72]

In the meantime, black recruits in the South were taken from states where the slave-holders were engaged in armed rebellion. Later in 1863, the administration began to look about for new fields in which to recruit blacks. Slaves in the exempted areas could not be taken without compensation to loyal masters. On 13 October 1863, in General Orders No. 329, the War Department established recruiting stations in Maryland, Tennessee, Missouri, and Delaware. These orders stated that all able-bodied free blacks, slaves of disloyal persons, and slaves of loyal persons with the consent of their owners were declared to be eligible for military employment. Counties and states furnishing black recruits were to be credited with them, and loyal masters consenting to the enlistment of their slaves were to receive three hundred dollars for each one, after filing proof of ownership and furnishing a deed of manumission.[73]

Ten months after the Emancipation Proclamation, there were fifty-eight regiments of black troops in the Union army with a total strength, including white officers, of 37,482 men. Training camps had been established, recruiting was taking place almost everywhere, and many units had already participated in combat action. By December 1863, over 50,000 blacks had been enrolled in the Union army and this number was rapidly increasing as Union troops moved deeper into the Confederacy. Before the end of the war, more than 200,000 blacks, most of them ex-slaves, served in the Union army and navy. General Lorenzo Thomas wrote in December 1863, concerning the 20,830 blacks he had enlisted up to that time, that the typical black volunteer made a dependable and resolute soldier. He was fighting for the Union, but he was also fighting to win a new dignity and self-respect, as well as for an America in which his children would have greater liberties and responsibilities. President Lincoln wrote General James S. Wadsworth, just one year after the Emancipation Proclamation, that the black troops had heroically vindicated their manhood on the battlefield.[74]

The exclusion of blacks from the armed forces worked only so long as the government and northern whites were confident they were going to win the war. After Fort Sumter, with patriotic whites rallying to the flag, there seemed little reason to doubt that the rebellion would be easily and quickly crushed. However, several months later, the expected quick victory did not materialize and the war was still raging with no end in sight. As the North suffered more and more adversities on the battlefield and, as casualties and desertions increased, the demand for employing blacks as soldiers increased. In the last analysis, however, blacks won the right to fight, not only by decisions made in Washington by the President, the Secretary of War, Congress, or even by generals on the battlefield, but by their own performance as soldiers in action.

A great expansion of black recruiting activity took place in 1864, but already in 1863 the policy of black enlistment had proved itself a success in both North and South. Black soldiers in 1863 fought courageously at Port Hudson, Milliken's Bend, Fort Wagner, and Moscow Station. However, black soldiers were still somewhat on an experimental basis; they were expected to make their contributions to the war mainly by providing a labor force for the armies and by garrisoning forts, thus relieving white troops for combat. But from the beginning of 1864, and throughout the remainder of the war, black soldiers became engaged in more and more combat. Circumstances had forced black regiments into combat and they demonstrated that they could perform with courage, skill, and determination.

26

CHAPTER II

BLACK SOLDIERS IN THE UNION ARMY

After the administration committed itself to the military employment of blacks as soldiers, following the Emancipation Proclamation, changes came very rapidly. Black regiments were organized, camps were established to train them, and recruiting took place almost everywhere. Blacks as a whole enlisted in the Union army with enthusiasm. In the North leading blacks like Frederick Douglass, Martin Delaney, and John Langston acted as recruiting agents. Rallies were held at which speakers urged blacks to enlist, and in city after city they went to the recruiting stations in large numbers.

In the South thousands of blacks also enlisted. However, the recruiting agents in the South often encountered frustrations and personal danger. Slaves were sometimes whipped, mutilated, and murdered for trying to enlist. Despite these problems, by the end of the war 134,111 were recruited or conscripted in the slave states. These southern blacks constituted a large majority of the total 186,017 black men who served in the Union army.[1]

With the official enlistment of black troops, the question of their treatment in the United States Army immediately arose. From the beginning the official policy was for blacks to serve in separate regiments commanded by white officers. But there were other questions that required answers, such as: (1) Would black soldiers receive equal pay? (2) If they were captured by the enemy, would they be treated as prisoners of war? (3) If they were maimed for life, would they receive pensions from the government? (4) Would blacks be engaged primarily in menial tasks instead of fighting? (5) Would they receive equal bounties and treatment? Many of these questions were never satisfactorily answered or resolved.[2]

At the beginning there was discrimination in the pay of white and black soldiers. White privates were paid $13 a month plus a $3.50 clothing allowance, while blacks of the same rank received only $7 and $3, respectively. Cities and states aided white soldiers' families, but little was done for families of black soldiers. Not until July 1864 did the federal

27

government make any provision for the wives and families of black soldiers who had been killed in action or had died of wounds or disease while in federal service.[3]

Secretary of War Edwin Stanton, in his annual report to Congress, in December 1863 asked for legislation to equalize the pay of white and black soldiers. Representative Thaddeus Stevens introduced such a bill, but opposition from conservative Democrats and Republicans delayed the measure. They argued that to pay blacks the same wages as white soldiers would degrade the white man. Equal pay to black soldiers would in effect place former slaves on the same level with freeborn northern whites, and this idea could hardly be tolerated by large segments of the northern population, particularly in the lower economic strata where competition with cheap black labor was both feared and hated. While politicians argued and Congress delayed, the families of black soldiers were suffering. Seven dollars per month was scarely enough to support a family, especially when the soldiers were not paid on time.[4]

Black soldiers and their spokesmen argued that, since black soldiers served with white soldiers, ate the same food, wore the same uniform, worked, fought, and died just as the whites did, they were entitled to the same pay. And since the black soldier performed his job at a substantially greater personal risk than his white contemporaries in the Union army, it seemed only minimum justice that he should be paid what the remainder of the Union army drew. Black spokesmen further argued that Secretary of War Stanton had promised black soldiers standard army pay in his original authorization to General Rufus Saxton, the first definite War Department authorization for the enrollment of blacks as soldiers.[5]

Black soldiers served under a further financial disadvantage. Until the middle of 1864, they were not entitled to receive the federal bounty of $100 granted to white volunteers from the third month of the war. Black recruits were denied this bounty even before their reception into the Union army had been authorized by the War Department. On 19 August 1862, Assistant Adjutant General Thomas Vincent notified Lieutenant Charles S. Bowmen, disbursing officer at Fort Leavenworth, Kansas, that recruits for black regiments would under no circumstances be paid bounty and premiums. General Benjamin Butler managed to secure War Department authority for a $10 bounty for black recruits in Virginia at the end of November 1863, but this was limited to his command.[6]

Colonel Thomas W. Higginson, the commander of the First South Carolina Volunteers (the first official black regiment mustered into the Union army), became one of the leading proponents of equal financial treatment of black soldiers. In a letter to the New York Tribune in January 1864, Higginson stated that every man in his regiment had volunteered under an explicit written assurance from the War Department that he would be paid the same as white soldiers. He further stated that his men would have served without pay if they were convinced that the government actually needed the money. Unfortunately, the black troops had seen white soldiers all around them receiving hundreds of dollars in bounties for re-enlisting in the government's army that paid them only $7 a month and no bounty. This inequality in financial treatment, according to Higginson, inflicted untold suffering, impaired discipline, relaxed loyalty, and implanted a feeling of distrust in the government.[7]

The inequality in pay assumed a significance for many black soldiers that went beyond the question of dollars and cents. This distinction branded them as second-class soldiers and citizens. Black soldiers objected vigorously to this discrimination. The Fifty-fourth and Fifty-fifth Massachusetts Regiments served a year without pay rather than accept discriminatory wages. Confronted with growing resentment of discrimination and the still pressing need to attract more recruits, black spokesmen on the home front pressed for equal rights in the army while at the same time they urged more enlistments.[8]

It was not until 15 June 1864 that Congress finally enacted legislation granting equal pay to black soldiers. The law was made retroactive to 1 January 1864 for all black soldiers, and retroactive to the time of enlistment for those blacks who had been free on 19 April 1861. On 18 August 1864, the adjutant general's office issued Circular 60 directing commanders of black regiments to find out which of their men had been free on 19 April 1861. This information was to be obtained from the soldiers' statements under oath and by other reliable sources available. This distinction between freemen and freedmen created a serious dilemma for some regiments because most northern black regiments had both free blacks and ex-slaves in their ranks. Morale in such regiments was impaired by some men receiving more back pay than others.[9]

The Confederacy was outraged by the northern use of black soldiers. The employment of armed slaves to fight white men provoked cries of disbelief. When Union generals began to recruit blacks as soldiers during mid-1862, most Southerners became very indignant. Most people in the South and Conferederate leaders regarded this as the beginning of a movement to turn the slaves of the entire South against their masters. Many thought the recruitment of blacks would incite slave revolts. The vast majority of Southerners viewed black soldiers as rebellious slaves and insisted that they should be treated as such. Confederate War Department General Orders, No. 60, issued 21 August 1862, stated the official attitude of the South toward Union officers that had begun to arm slaves. These officers would be treated as outlaws and when captured would not be regarded as prisoners of war, but held in close confinement for execution as felons at the time and place prescribed by the President.[10] The Confederate government felt that the best means of repressing the crime of raising black troops against it was the outlawing of all persons guilty of that crime. And, to most people of the South, arming slaves was a heinous crime.[11]

A few months later President Jefferson David extended General Orders No. 60. When the Union began to recruit black regiments in the Mississippi Valley, Davis directed his Secretary of War, James A. Seddon, to inform the commanding officers in the area that captured black soldiers should not be regarded as prisoners of war and should be turned over to state authorities and treated in accordance with the laws of the state in which they had been taken prisoners. This punishment was the equivalent of a death sentence since the law in every one of the seceded states branded such blacks as incendiaries and insurrectionists.[12]

The publication of Lincoln's preliminary Emancipation Proclamation on 22 September 1862 and its final form on 1 January 1863 aroused President Davis and the Confederacy to an indignation which had no bounds. Davis stated to the Confederate Congress that Lincoln's proclamation would result in the extermination of several million human beings of an inferior race who were peaceful and contented laborers. He further stated that he would deliver to the state authorities all commissioned officers of the United States who were captured by Confederate forces to be treated in accordance with the laws of those states providing for the punishment of criminals engaged in exciting servile insurrection.[13]

On 1 May 1863, the Confederate Congress passed a resolution which directed that commissioned officers commanding, arming, training, organizing, or preparing blacks for military service in the United States Army should be put to death or brought before a military court for punishment if captured. The black soldiers should be delivered to the authorities of the states in which they were captured to be treated according to the laws of that state.[14] Since the sessions of the Confederate Congress were usually conducted in secret, the general public for several months did not know what actions it had taken regarding black soldiers.[15]

The news of the position of President and the Confederate Congress toward black soldiers and their commanders resulted in an outcry from some Union generals and northern people. In a letter to President Lincoln, General David Hunter stated that the flag should protect and cover all its defenders irrespective of their color, and suggested that in retaliation all Confederate prisoners, particularly those of the aristocratic caste, should be held as hostages to be hung man for man with any who might be executed by the Confederates. Disliking an eye-for-an-eye policy, Lincoln at first thought of limiting the employment of blacks to places sufficiently removed from the war fronts to prevent their being captured.[16]

Events during June and July 1863 brought the black prisoner problem more to the forefront. As the number of black regiments increased and became more involved in combat, persistent reports came of the murdering and selling into slavery of captured black soldiers. The Confederate government denied the alleged murdering of black soldiers and promised a full investigation. But it consistently contended that slaves captured in arms should be returned to their masters. However, some Southerners did agree that the Union might employ northern blacks as soldiers. Union officials argued that slaves became free men when they entered the United States military and were protected by the United States government; therefore, they could

31

not be re-enslaved even by their former owners. They insisted that all captured black soldiers should be treated as prisoners of war.[17]

Union generals, the press, and many northern people began to demand a formal statement of policy from President Lincoln concerning the black prisoner problem. General Ulysses S. Grant declared if any of his soldiers, black or white, wearing the uniform of the United States were captured and executed retaliatory measures would be taken by him against Confederate soldiers. Frederick Douglass refused to continue his recruiting efforts and stated that his faith in Lincoln was nearly gone. Under pressure, Lincoln reacted on 30 July 1863. He ordered that for every Union soldier killed in violation of the laws of war a Confederate soldier would be executed, and for every one enslaved by the enemy or sold into slavery a Confederate soldier would be placed at hard labor on the public works and continued at such labor until the other shall be released and receive the treatment due to a prisoner of war. Lincoln's action in ordering retaliation was generally hailed with approval in the North and by several Union newspapers in the South.[18]

The official position of the Union and Confederate governments on the treatment of captured soldiers resulted in a deadlock. The Confederacy would not retreat from its extreme position of the congressional resolution. The Union was now committed to Lincoln's policy of retaliation for whatever acts the Confederate government should commit in line with that resolution. The immediate result was a breakdown in the cartel for the exchange of prisoners. The southern press, representing southern opinion, stated that no exchange of prisoners would take place other than soldier for soldier. Ex-slaves who had taken up arms against their masters would not be treated as prisoners of war and, therefore, would not be exchanged against white men.[19]

General Benjamin Butler was appointed a special agent of prisoner exchange under Ethan A. Hitchcock in December 1863. Butler later met with Judge Robert Ould, the Confederate commissioner of prisoner exchange. Ould did agree that all free blacks could be treated as prisoners of war, but would not agree on recaptured slaves. He reiterated that slaves were property and that property recaptured from an enemy in war reverts to its owner if he can be found or may be disposed of by its captor in any way he sees proper. With increasing military activities in mid-1864, discussions broke down completely.[20]

In some cases Confederate officers refused to take black prisoners. Those who were not sold into slavery were murdered in cold blood after capture. The so-called "Fort Pillow Massacre" was the most notable instance of the murder of black prisoners after capture. Fort Pillow was a Union outpost on the Mississippi River about forty miles from Memphis, Tennessee. It was garrisoned by approximately 570 troops, of whom slightly less than half were black, under the command of Major L. F. Booth. On 12 April 1864, Confederate General Nathan B. Forrest, commanding a division of cavalrymen, demanded its surrender. After several hours of fighting the fort fell to Forrest's forces. According to testimonies, more than 300 soldiers, mostly blacks, were murdered after they had surrendered.[21]

George W. Williams states that as rapidly as the men surrendered they were murdered. Many black soldiers, who realized that no mercy would be shown them, rushed down the bluff to the river to escape, but were pursued by the enemy and shot. The Confederate soldiers' yell was "no quarters." He further states that women and children of the garrison, white and black, young and old, mistress and servant, were shot down with indiscriminate inhumanity.[22]

This incident at Fort Pillow, Tennessee, provoked the most bitter black protest of the Civil War. There were also reports of the shooting of captured and wounded black soldiers in the battles of Poison Spring, Arkansas, and Petersburg, Virginia. It is impossible to state how many black soldiers and their officers lost their lives because of Confederate policy. The Fort Pillow Massacre induced black troops to fight with even greater ferocity and determination; some of them were apparently convinced capture was equivalent to murder. Some black soldiers took an oath to avenge Fort Pillow and as they assaulted Confederate lines their battle cry became, "Remember Fort Pillow."[23]

President Lincoln and his cabinet considered the Fort Pillow case in early May. Recommendations for action varied. Secretary of State William Seward suggested that Confederate

prisoners be confined as hostages until their government either
explained or disavowed the massacre and pledged against
repetition. Secretary of War Edwin Stanton advised that
Confederate officers be held as hostages, that General Forrest
and all members of his command involved in the affair be
excluded from amnesty and exchange, and that their delivery for
punishment be demanded of the Confederate government. If the
government refused, Lincoln should take action against the
officer hostages. Secretary of Interior John P. Usher and
Attorney General Edward Bates condemned retaliation on innocent
men, but urged the prisoners taken from Forrest's command be
held for execution. Very little action, however, came from
these discussions.[24]

Black soldiers were also subjected to many indignities and
injustices by the Union. A disproportionate number of blacks
were often assigned to heavy labor and fatigue duty. Blacks
were unrepresented in court-martial proceedings and excluded
from military academies. Few blacks could hope to become
officers. Although 186,017 blacks were enlisted during the war,
less than one hundred held commissions in the Union army, and
most of them were in the Louisiana militia taken into federal
service in 1862. The strong doubt that existed on qualifications
of black soldiers for military life made it difficult for them to
secure commissions.[25]

The contributions of black soldiers were remarkable
considering the disadvantages under which they served. They
were placed in segregated units under white officers who were
often prejudiced. Many officers in white regiments were given
command of black regiments as a reward for gallantry and
meritorious service in the field, or on account of proficiency in
drill. Thus, many officers assigned to black regiments were not
well trained, though many were brave. Black regiments went
into battle with less training than the white regiments had
received and with weapons inferior to those issued to whites.
The ordnance department often sent arms and equipment to blac
units that were either obsolete or faultily constructed. Most
white regiments were issued the new model Springfield rifles,
considered among the best in the world at the time. In 1864 the
army adopted the Spencer breech-loading repeating rifle which
fired fourteen rounds a minute and issued it to white regiments.[26]

Medical care, inadequate for whites, was even worse for blacks. In black units there was a serious shortage of surgeons. It was not easy to induce medical officers to accept commissions in black regiments. In many cases hospital stewards of inferior qualification were appointed to the office of assistant surgeon and surgeon. Well-grounded objections were made from every quarter against the inhumanity of subjecting the black soldiers to medical treatment and surgical operations from these men. The available black physicians faced hardships if they attempted to serve. They were often attacked by white soldiers because of their rank, they seldom got paid on time, and some paymasters insisted that they should be paid $7 a month, the same as the black soldiers were paid before 15 June 1864. Only eight black physicians were appointed surgeons in the army; six of them were attached to hospitals in Washington, D.C., while the other two remained with black regiments for only a very short time. Blacks suffered greater casualties than whites for all of these reasons. Approximately one-third of the black soldiers--an estimated 68,178--were listed as dead and missing.[27]

As the federal government took some action to correct obvious injustices toward blacks in the Union army, there were disturbing signs of white backlash. Thousands of white northern soldiers engaged in constant harassment and open hostility toward black troops. As late as 1864, white mobs in the North often assaulted off-duty black soldiers. Several serious race riots occurred in 1862-63. These riots were sparked by job competition between white and black laborers and by the white workingman's fear that emancipation would cause a flood of blacks on the labor market and drive down wages. There was also opposition to the new federal draft law of March 1863. Following the draft law, a white mob in Detroit invaded the black section of that city shouting that if whites had to fight for blacks they would kill every black in town. They did kill several and destroyed thirty-two houses, which left more than two hundred people homeless. In New York City a protest against the draft turned into an orgy of race hatred. Dozens of blacks were lynched in the streets or murdered in their homes. Federal troops were called in to restore order.[28]

The overall performance of black soldiers is deserving of high commendation despite the disadvantages under which they served. Many in the North and South were surprised to find that blacks, especially those who had been slaves, made good soldiers. In more than 450 minor and major battles, they fought bravely and won praise from both friends and enemies. Black soldiers were organized in 120 infantry regiments, 12 heavy artillery regiments, 10 light artillery batteries, and 7 cavalry regiments. Seventeen blacks won the Congressional Medal of Honor. One year after the Emancipation Proclamation, President Lincoln stated that the black troops had heroically vindicated their manhood on the battlefield.[29]

Black soldiers saw action in every theater of operation during the Civil War. The first major offensive launched by black troops occurred 27 May 1863 at Port Hudson, Louisiana. Some 1,080 members of the First and Third Regiments of the Louisiana Native Guards formed the right wing of a Union assaulting force against the 6,000-man Confederate garrison. The blacks attacked one of the strongest natural positions along the Mississippi River. The conduct of these men, even in defeat, surprised their most vocal critics. The First Regiment was composed of free blacks while the Third Regiment was composed mostly of ex-slaves, and nearly two-thirds of the two regiments' line officers were black. The records indicate that these black officers gave their men the leadership the assaults demanded. Captain Andre Cailloux, commanding Company E of the First Regiment, stood out as the individual hero of the assaults, although at the cost of his life. Six desperate charges were made by these black troops, and, after it was evident that it was not lack of courage on their part, they were ordered to withdraw.[30]

In a letter to General Henry Halleck, General Nathaniel Banks stated that, "whatever doubts may have existed heretofore as to the efficiency of black regiments," their performance at Port Hudson "proves conclusively" to observers that black troops will provide effective defenders for the government. He concluded that "the severe test to which they were subjected, and the determined manner in which they encountered the enemy, leaves upon my mind no doubt of their ultimate success."[31]

Before the news of Port Hudson reached Washington, two other Louisiana black regiments distinguished themselves at Milliken's Bend, a Union camp in Louisiana about twenty miles upstream from Vicksburg, a Confederate stronghold. A detachment of about 1,000 men, of whom 160 were white and the remainder were exslaves from Louisiana and Mississippi, were organized into two regiments, the Ninth and Eleventh Louisiana. They were left in defense of this important Union camp. On 7 June 1863, a Confederate division of about 2,000 soldiers, under the command of General J. G. Walker and General Henry E. McCulloch, launched an assault on Milliken's Bend. For hours the two sides fought in close combat with bayonets and muskets. Union forces were pushed to the Mississippi riverbank. But they later received reinforcements from two Union gunboats, the Lexington and Choctaw, that bombarded the Confederates into withdrawal.[32]

General Elias S. Dennis, commanding the Union forces, described the battle as the hardest he had ever seen. It was fought mainly hand to hand. After it was over, many men were found dead with bayonet stabs, and others with their skulls broken open by butts of muskets. Captain Matthew M. Miller of Company I, Ninth Louisiana, who lost sixteen killed and fifteen wounded of his original thirty-three men described the battle as horrible, the worst in which he was ever engaged, including Shiloh. The enemy cried, "no quarters," but some of them were glad to take it when made prisoners. The Ninth Louisiana lost 62 killed and 130 wounded; the Eleventh, 30 killed and 120 wounded. General Dennis stated that it was impossible for men to show greater gallantry than the black troops in this fight.[33] George W. Williams states that the battle of Milliken's Bend will always rank as one of the hardest fought actions of the Civil War, and the unimpeachable valor of the black troops will remain a priceless heritage of the race for whose freedom they nobly contended.[34]

On 17 July 1863, at Elk Creek near Honey Springs in Indian territory, Union General James G. Blunt attacked Confederate General Douglas Cooper. In this largest engagement in the territory, the Confederates fled after a bloody engagement of more than two hours. At Honey Springs the First Kansas Colored Regiment established its military reputation. During the fight the First Kansas, which held the Union center, moved up under fire to within fifty paces of the Confederate line and there, still under fire, halted and exchanged volley fire for some thirty minutes until the Texans and their Indian allies broke and ran. The black regiment captured the colors of a Texas regiment. This was the most important battle in the regiment's entire history.

37

General Blunt stated that he never saw such fighting before. The soldiers fought like veterans, with a coolness and valor that were unsurpassed. They preserved their line perfectly throughout the whole engagement and, although in the hottest of the fight, they never once faltered. Too much praise cannot be awarded for their gallantry. General Blunt further stated that these black soldiers were the best he ever had under his command.[35]

One of the most famous black assaults of the war took place 18 July 1863 at Fort Wagner on Morris Island, South Carolina. The Fifty-fourth Massachusetts Regiment (the first black northern regiment to go to war) was ordered to launch an assault against the fort. This was the first major battle for the Union troops in the Department of the South. Most of the Sea Islands had fallen to the control of the Union forces, but the way to Charleston, both by land and water, was guarded by forts, fortifications, and torpedoes. Fort Wagner was a strongly mounted and thoroughly garrisoned earthwork extending across the north end of the island; it was within twenty-six hundred yards of Fort Sumter.[36]

The Fifty-fourth Regiment had been marching through sand and swamps for most of the day before the 6:00 P.M. assault. They had fought on James Island on 16 July and had sustained a loss of fourteen killed, seventeen wounded, and thirteen missing. They had gone two nights without rest and two days without rations. Colonel Robert Shaw, commander of the Fifty-fourth, reported to General George Strong on Morris Island on the afternoon of 18 July. General Strong offered the Fifty-fourth the honor of leading the assault. Having complained in a letter to General Strong that he wanted better service and not more guerrilla warfare for his soldiers, Shaw could not refuse this supreme chance to prove the valor of his regiment. The hand-to-hand fighting that resulted was vicious. Colonel Shaw and three other officers of the Fifty-fourth were killed. The Union momentarily gained a toehold, but lost after frightful casualties. Sergeant William H. Carney became the first black soldier to win the Congressional Medal of Honor for valor during the Battle of Fort Wagner.[37]

According to George Williams, Colonel Shaw led about 600 enlisted men and 22 officers into this action. Of the enlisted men 31 were killed, 135 wounded, and 92 missing. Of the 22 officers participating 3 were killed and 11 were wounded. Nearly

38

half of the enlisted men were killed, wounded, or missing, while more than one-half of the officers were either killed or wounded. This appalling list of casualties shows how bravely this regiment performed its duty. [38]

Hardly another black operation of the war received so much publicity or stirred so much comment. Colonel Shaw and the Fifty-fourth became symbols of the best that troops, white or black, could do. After the assault on Fort Wagner, there was no longer any doubt about using black troops to crush the rebellion. Joseph Holt, Judge Advocate General and former Secretary of War, wrote Edwin M. Stanton in August 1863: "The tenacious and brilliant valor displayed by troops of this race at Port Hudson, Milliken's, and Fort Wagner has sufficiently demonstrated to the President and to the country the character of the service of which they are capable." [39]

Between May 1863 and March 1864, the Union army at Memphis recruited and organized some 6,957 black men into seven infantry regiments, three heavy artillery regiments, and two batteries of light artillery. Additionally, the Third United States Colored Cavalry Regiment was organized in Memphis and stationed at Vicksburg and in 1865 at Memphis. The black troops in West Tennessee were stationed mostly along the vital rail lines, rivers, and bridges. Though by the summer of 1862 the Union army controlled West Tennessee, the Confederate forces maintained control of east-central Mississippi from where they periodically raided the rural western part of Tennessee. The whites of the area generally supported the Confederate cause. The Union, therefore, organized thousands of blacks into military units in an attempt to check the guerrilla raids of the vital rail and communication lines which connected Memphis southward to Union-held Corinth and Vicksburg, as well as those lines which connected northward to Nashville and the northern states. During the fall of 1863, Confederate forces under General Stephen D. Lee infiltrated the area just thirty-eight miles east of Memphis. Because the black regiments had not begun to organize until May 1863, the Confederates were surprised to encounter them guarding the vital rail lines. When Lee's men tested the raw black recruits of the Second Colored West Tennessee Infantry (later renamed the Sixty-first United States Colored Troops Infantry Regiment) with sniper fire, the blacks stood their ground and returned the fire. [40]

The first serious engagement between black troops and West Tennessee Confederate forces was at the Battle of Moscow on 3-4 December 1863. On 3 December, Union reinforcements arrived to help buttress the defenses of the vital bridge at Moscow which spanned the Wolf River and served as a passage for the Memphis-Charleston railroad. The Confederates, at 3:00 P.M., directed heavy fire on the Union guards, but the reinforced garrison was able to force the enemy to withdraw near nightfall. Around noon the next day more Union troops arrived including companies from the Sixty-first Colored Regiment and a detachment from the Second Colored Light Artillery. The Confederate forces attacked for a second time that afternoon. The black soldiers led by the Second Infantry and Artillery forced the Confederates to retreat after a major engagement, and the two sides engaged in shooting and shelling each other from opposite river banks. The black artillery's accuracy in throwing shells right into the midst of the Confederate ranks and causing them to retreat surprised even their own officers.[41]

Colonel Frank Kendrick, regimental commander, and other white Union officers applauded the combat behavior of the black troops at the battle of Moscow. After General Stephen A. Hulburt, the corps commander, had received full reports from subordinate commanders speaking highly of the soldierly qualities evinced by the Second Infantry and other blacks at Moscow, he was moved to issue a general order commending them. General Orders No. 173 (17 December 1863) stated that the recent affair at Moscow, Tennessee, had demonstrated the fact that black troops, properly disciplined and commanded, can and will fight well. Hulburst personally commended the black troops for their gallant and successful defense of the important position to which they had been assigned, and for the manner in which they had vindicated the wisdom of the government in elevating the rank and file of these regiments to the position of freedmen and soldiers.[42]

As 1863 drew to a close the procedure and machinery for recruiting black troops were thoroughly developed. In his annual report to the President in early December, Secretary of War Edwin Stanton reported that over 50,000 blacks had already been organized as Union soldiers and that the number would rapidly increase as Union armies advanced into the Confederate states. There was no doubt in Stanton's mind about the practicality of the full military employment of blacks. He maintained they had proved their ability as infantrymen, artillerymen, and cavalrymen.[43]

President Lincoln was also satisfied that the policy of drawing on the black manpower of the nation for soldiers was proving successful. He reported in his third annual message to Congress that 100,000 blacks who were slaves at the beginning of the rebellion were in the United States military service. He further stated that about one-half of the 100,000 blacks were under arms, thus giving the double advantage of taking labor from the Confederates and adding them to the Union in places which otherwise would be filled with white men.[44]

However, by the end of 1863, War Department efforts to organize black regiments were hampered by a lack of able officers to train and command the black recruits. Up to 26 December 1863 a total of 1,051 applicants had come before the examining boards, and of these 560 had passed while 491, or almost 47 percent, had been rejected. War Department General Orders Nos. 143 and 144 issued on 22 May 1863 had established the Bureau for Colored Troops. Number 143 directed that boards be set up to examine applicants for commissions to command black troops. These boards also had authority over the selection of recruiting officers for black troops, as well as over appointments to line and field positions.[45]

General Order No. 144 prescribed rules to guide the boards. They were required to examine only applicants with approval from the Adjutant General to appear before them. To gain this permission, an applicant was required to present satisfactory recommendations of good moral character and standing in the community in which he lived or, if a soldier, he must have testimonials from his commanding officers. These recommendations had to be filed in advance with the Bureau for Colored Troops. Each applicant was to receive a fair but rigorous examination as to physical, mental, and moral fitness to command troops. The boards also specified the grade of commission each approved applicant would have.[46]

The appearance before these examining boards was not considered an easy matter by the officers and men of the Union army or by civilians eligible to try for commissions in black regiments. The strictness of the boards was indicative of the fact that roughly forty-seven percent of all who attempted the examinations in 1863 were rejected. The War Department became concerned over this situation and out of this concern came the forerunner of the Officer Candidate School, a free military academy to prepare candidates for the ordeal of meeting the board.[47]

General Silas Casey, president of the Washington examining board, suggested to the Philadelphia Supervisory Committee for Recruiting Colored Regiments that a few weeks of concentrated study on tactics and army regulations would enable more candidates for commissions to pass the board. Thomas Webster, chairman of the Philadelphia committee, accepted the suggestion, secured a faculty, published a prospectus, devised a thirty-day course of study, and on 26 December 1863 opened a school for applicants for the command of colored troops. Within two months, the school was operating and doing an effective job. On 7 March 1864, General Casey wrote Chairman Webster to congratulate him on the success of the enterprise and to inform him that his Washington board had yet to reject one of the school's graduates. The school attracted wide attention in a short time. The War Department later issued General Orders No. 125 that permitted furloughs, not to exceed thirty days, to the non-commissioned officers and privates of the army who desired to enter the military school at Philadelphia when the character, conduct, and capacity of the applicants were such as to warrant their immediate and superior commanders in recommending them for commissioned appointments in the regiments of black troops. The Philadelphia school was geared into the army's machinery and played a large role in the preparation and selection of officers for black troops.[48]

By the spring of 1864, a great change had taken place in getting officers for the black regiments. At the end of April there were 513 candidates recommended for commissions by the various examining boards and awaiting appointments. There were several reasons for seeking a commission in the black regiments aside from the more obvious advantages of social distinction, better pay, better food, and quarters. There was the realistic consideration of increased chance of survival. It was calculated that the proportionate Civil War battle losses of enlisted men to officers was sixteen to one and the officers were far less likely to succumb to the fatalities of disease than were their men. The rigid examination was another motivating factor for many to seek commissions in black regiments, because it produced leaders substantially better qualified than those who led the white volunteer army in the first two years of the war. Many commanders of black troops recognized not only their military responsibilities to the men of their regiments, but went even further to help those men prepare for the lives they would lead as free men after the war was over. Such officers as Thomas W. Higginson, James Beecher, Thomas J. Morgan, Robert G. Shaw, Norwood P. Hallowell, and Daniel Ullmann set high standards of personal leadership and strove night and day to look after their men, to train them as soldiers, and to teach them to read and write. However, not all of the more than seven thousand officers who led the black troops were paragons of virtue and courage or even intelligence.[49]

After serving their apprenticeship in 1863 with distinction, it became logical and natural that black soldiers would find themselves more and more in action in 1864. Black soldiers had given definite indications during their combat performance in 1863 of what could be expected of them. If doubt still remained in some minds as to the fighting ability of black soldiers, their combat performance during 1864 and 1865 should have removed a great deal. It is obviously impossible to discuss every engagement in which black troops fought during these years and to analyze their varying behavior in action. Only a few of the battles, major and minor, will be discussed and they must stand as representative of the whole.[50]

In the Battle of Olustee, or Ocean Pond, near Jacksonville, Florida, on 20 February 1864, three black and six white regiments (plus smaller artillery and cavalry units) under the command of General Thomas Seymour engaged in a major battle against Confederate forces. The three black infantry regiments were the Eighth, the First North Carolina (subsequently the Thirty-fifth), and the famed Fifty-fourth Massachusetts. With a force of about 5,000 men, General Seymour encountered a much larger Confederate force. The Confederate forces awaited the Union forces from behind earthworks extending through heavy timber and impassable swamps. The Union forces were weary and hungry, having marched sixteen miles over heavy roads and through numerous swamps before the surprise engagement. The Union was defeated after a very stubborn fight. According to reports of the officers in charge of the black regiments, the First North Carolina and the Fifty-fourth Massachusetts behaved creditably, like veterans. Sergeant Stephen A. Swails was cited for bravery and efficiency despite a severe wound. He later became the first black to be commissioned in the Fifty-fourth. The Eighth Regiment performed well considering the fact that it was a new regiment and its men had never been in action before, but it lost more than 300 out of 550 men. The total black casualties were 503, over one-fourth of the total Union casualties, in what was the major battle of the war in Florida.[51]

Although the Battle of Olustee was not a victory for the Union, it furnished another opportunity for martial valor of the highest order on the part of the black soldiers. This was one of the severest battles of the war and if it had not been for the stubborn fighting of these black troops General Seymour would have been routed and annihilated. The stubborn tenacity of black soldiers was motivated in part by their awareness that as prisoners they had no rights which the Confederates respected. In explaining his defeat General Seymour reported that the black troops behaved creditably. He further stated that their conduct was not the chief cause of failure, but the unanticipated yielding of a white regiment (Seventh New Hampshire) from which there was every reason to expect noble service.[52]

The Virginia theater, more than any other, witnessed the action of many black soldiers during the last year of the war. By far the greatest number of black troops in any single theater of the war were involved in the slow bloody work of wearing down the Army of Northern Virginia from May 1864 through April 1865. General Ulysses S. Grant, now general-in-chief of the Union forces, transferred nearly twenty thousand black troops from other areas to the armies of the James and the Potomac. In addition to these black troops, there were in Virginia and Maryland a host of recently recruited black troops ready to assist in the final thrusts designed to defeat General Robert E. Lee's veteran army and capture Richmond. These new black recruits had trained during the winter of 1863-64 at Camp Stanton in Annapolis, Maryland, under General Ambrose Burnside and in Virginia under General Benjamin Butler.[53]

On 7 April 1864, General Burnside's Ninth Army Corps left camp and crossed the Potomac. During May and June, Burnside's black soldiers fought north of Richmond; the blacks in the Army of the James, commanded by General Butler, fought south of Richmond. In mid-June General Grant decided to make an attack on Peterburg, Virginia, a vitally important railroad center, twenty-two miles below Richmond. General William F. Smith and the Eighteenth Corp were ordered to attack on 15 June 1864. One of Smith's three divisions was a black brigade of about three thousand men, under the command of General Edward Hinks, consisting of four infantry regiments, two cavalry regiments, and two batteries. The Fifth and Twenty-second black regiments cleared the enemy's outpost for the attack by the entire corps. The black division was ordered to attack the main line of the Confederate works. To reach their assigned position eight hundred yards away, the black soldiers had to advance across an open field, exposed the whole distance to deadly fire. After over five hours, their ordeal ended as they gained their position, having advanced a few nerve-racking rods at a time. For five more hours they lay in the shadow of Confederate guns, while General Smith made a reconnaissance preparatory to launching the general assault. Finally the charge was ordered. The fighting that followed was devastating. Both sides suffered heavy losses as the Confederate forces retreated.[54]

The black soldiers again proved their gallantry and amazed their fellow white soldiers who were very vocal in their expressions of admiration. The Leavenworth Daily Conservative reported from Virginia that the hardest fighting was done by the black troops. The forts they stormed were the worst of all. General Smith praised the conduct of his black troops in his report of the action, and in a proclamation of appreciation he called them to the attention of the entire corps. The proclamation stated that the black soldiers had stormed the works of the enemy and carried them, taken guns and prisoners, and in the whole affair they had displayed all the qualities of good soldiers. General Smith further stated that the blacks could not be excelled as soldiers and hereafter he would send them to difficult places as readily as the best white troops. When Lincoln visited General Grant's camp six days later to review the Virginia commands, Grant suggested that they ride over and see the black troops who behaved so handsomely in Smith's attack on the works in front of Petersburg.[55]

Despite the bravery of the black soldiers, however, Petersburg was not taken. General Smith failed to follow up the success of the day's fighting. He bivouacked for the night, despite a clear sky and nearly full moon. Instead of marching his troops into Petersburg, General Smith waited for reinforcements unnecessarily, thereby losing his chance of taking the city, which was soon garrisoned with troops enough to later defy the whole army. From 16 June until the explosion of the mine on 30 July the black troops participated in the various duties of building fortifications, skirmishing, picket-duty, and sharp-shooting. In all these they performed their duty cheerfully, and won the confidence of the entire army. There were other black troops arriving daily, and they were distributed through the Ninth, Tenth, and Eighteenth corps in the Army of the Potomac and in the Army of the James.[56]

General Grant regarded Petersburg as the citadel of Richmond, and its capture was very important to him. Encamped one hundred fifty yards from the enemy, the Union forces were confronted by a fort projecting beyond the Confederates' main line. If this outlying bastion were reduced, an assault on Petersburg could be launched. To achieve this end, the Union decided to run a mine under the fort and blow it up. The idea for the mine came from Colonel Henry Pleasants of the Forty-eighth Pennsylvania Regiment. Colonel Pleasants, a mining engineer before the war, convinced General Burnside and it was ultimately approved by General Grant. Colonel Pleasants' regiment, composed largely of coal miners from the Schuylkill Valley, began work on 25 June. Screened from the enemy's observation, the regiment worked steadily for five weeks, digging a five hundred eighty-six foot-long tunnel under the unsuspecting Confederates and charging the mine with eight thousand pounds of gunpowder. The tunnel averaged five feet in height, was four and a half feet wide at the bottom, and about two feet at the top. It was ventilated by an ingenious system whereby fire in a chimney near the entrance drew stale air out of the tunnel, while the resulting vacuum pulled fresh air through a wooden tube that ran along the floor of the tunnel from under a door at the entrance to the end where the men were digging.[57]

The plan of attack called for General Burnside's Ninth Corps to charge through the gap caused by the explosion of the mine on 30 July. They would then sweep along the enemy's line, right and left, clearing away the artillery and infantry. The crucial question was which of the four divisions of the Ninth Corps would lead the attack. General Edward Ferrero, commander of the black Fourth Division, was informed that he would lead the assault after the mine had been fired. He was ordered to drill his troops accordingly. When Ferrero informed his officers and men that they had been selected to lead the assault, they received the information with delight. They were all pleased with the compliment of being chosen to lead the assault. For three weeks they drilled with alacrity in the various movements, charging upon earthworks, and wheeling by the right and left. They also practiced deployment and other details of the expected operations.[58]

On 28 July, General George G. Meade had an interview with General Burnside and the plan of the assault was fully discussed. General Meade objected to the black division leading the assault. He felt that the black troops were not sufficiently seasoned to lead the assault and, if the venture failed, it would be said that the blacks were selected to lead the assault because of racism. But that could not be said if white troops led the assault. General Burnside argued with all the reason he could command in favor of his plans, especially for the blacks leading the assault. He argued that his white troops were unfit for performing the task of leading the attack. He reminded General Meade that his three white divisions had for forty days been in the trenches in the immediate presence of the enemy. Burnsides's argument, however, was in vain. The plan, with General Meade's objection, was referred to General Grant for settlement. General Grant was the supreme commander, but General Meade was in command of the Army of the Potomac. Grant, following military propriety, upheld Commander Meade, although later in his testimony before the Committee on the Conduct of the War, he confessed that he believed that if Burnside's recommendation had been followed the assault would have been successful.[59]

It was not until the night of the 29th, a few hours before the assault was made, that the change was made known to General Ferrero and his men. They were greatly chagrined and disappointed. Burnside ordered the three white divisions to draw straws for the lead position. General James H. Ledlie, commander of the battle-weary First Division that was lacking in strength, drew the short straw. Time permitted only a brief reconnaissance of the position, and that occurred after dark on the night of the 29th.[60]

The explosion was set for 3:30 A.M. on 30 July, but the fuse failed to work. At 4:15 two brave volunteers of the Forty-eighth Pennsylvania crawled into the tunnel and relit the fuse, which had burned out at the splice. At 4:45 the mine exploded. Colonel Pleasants' part of the work was a complete success as the explosion created a crater 170 feet long, 60 to 80 feet wide, and 30 feet deep; four Confederate companies were stattered by the eruption and partly buried in the debris. Simultaneously the Union guns, one hundred cannon and fifty mortars, opened up all along the line, and the First Division was ordered to charge. As the soldiers moved toward the crater, some fatal errors became apparent. These white troops, worn down by the constant campaigning in the weeks just preceding the assault, were unprepared by any special training or even instructions for the task. They did not move promptly enough to the attack. They milled about in confusion in the huge crater. The element of surprise was diminished by the delay, and the Confederates recovered much more quickly than anticipated. As more Union troops herded into the crater they were pounded by Confederate artillery.[61]

The black division was finally ordered to charge into the crater at about 7:30 after the three veteran white divisions had been hurled back in confusion. Faced by fire in front and a crossfire from the flanks, the black troops moved forward rapidly until they engaged the enemy in close combat. Many of their officers were killed and they suffered heavy casualties. Again and again they charged, but the Confederates held firmly, and after exhibiting great courage and sustaining severe casualties the blacks were recalled. The Confederates held their position. The whole operation cost the Union side almost four thousand men. The Fourth Black Division suffered the heaviest casualties. Confederate casualties were listed at fifteen hundred. The second major frontal assault on Petersburg had failed. In the aftermath, many charges, including ineffectiveness and drunkenness, were bandied about. At any rate, the successful mining operations ended in the failure of the assault because of Confederate resistance and some Union ineptitude.[62]

Newspaper accounts of the black troops in the Petersburg fiasco were divided along political lines. The Leavenworth Conservative gave credit to the black soldiers for bravery in the face of furious Confederate fire. The Putnam County Courier, a Democratic weekly published at Carmel, New York, stated that the blacks had fallen back in confusion, repulsed and demoralized. In his testimony before the seventeen-day court of inquiry, Burnside stated that the black soldiers went into the crater late, found it in a state of confusion, and during their advance they were subjected to probably the hottest fire that any troops had been subjected to during the day. He further stated that it would be unreasonable to expect them to have maintained their positions perfectly after the loss of so many of their officers. "They certainly moved forward as gallantly under the first fire and until their ranks were broken as any troops I ever saw in action," Burnside reported. [63]

The crater experience by no means demoralized the black soldiers in the Virginia theater. At Deep Bottom, Virginia, two weeks later, four black regiments incorporated into the Tenth Corps distinguished themselves under General David Birney, the corps commander. In this action at Deep Bottom from the 14–18 August 1864, black troops fought the enemy behind his intrenchments. On the night of 18 August the Confederates took the offensive and assaulted General Birney's troops vigorously, but his black soldiers were cool and determined, meeting the blow with courage. General Birney reported later that his black troops "behaved handsomely and were in fine spirits." [64]

On 29 September 1864, General Butler dispatched General Birney's Tenth Corps and the Eighteenth Corps under General Edward Ord across the James River. The country through which they passed were heavily wooded and hilly. The Confederates' outposts were struck and hurled back in confusion. During the afternoon, Birney's black division participated in an assault on Fort Gilmer, a Confederate earthwork near Chaffin's farm, which was unsuccessful. Confederate fire was fierce and worst of all, immediately before Fort Gilmer was a ditch, seven to ten feet deep, twice as broad, which turned into a death trap. Although the black troops attempted to move forward, standing on each other's shoulders to reach the edge of the parapet, rifle fire at point-blank range and hand grenades that rolled down among them soon forced their retreat. On the following day a successful assault was staged against Fort Harrison. Fort Harrison occupied a commanding position overlooking the James River only about five miles from Richmond. A considerable number of prisoners and guns were taken, and the Union flag was planted on Fort Harrison by black troops. The capture of Fort Harrison was a great manace to Richmond and the Confederates were determined to retake it. On 30 September, the Confederates hurled an assault of several divisions against Fort Harrison. The black troops held their ground and inflicted great punishment upon the enemy, who was routed and beaten off with severe loss. The position thus gained was held until the close of the war. This two-day engagement or series of engagements are known as the battles of Chaffin's Farm. Thirteen black regiments fought at Chaffin's Farm in Virginia. A total of thirty-seven Congressional Medals of Honor were awarded to soldiers of these battles; fourteen went to black soldiers.[65]

The black soldiers saw their share of action in nearly all the military engagements around Richmond and Petersburg during 1864. These battles convinced even the reluctant General Benjamin F. Butler that black soldiers could handle themselves creditably in any kind of action. General Grant, Secretary of War Stanton, and President Lincoln were very impressed with the performance of the black troops throughout 1864. They were so impressed with their performance that the Twenty-fifth Army Corps was organized by the War Department on 3 December 1864 from the black troops of the Department of Virginia and North Carolina under General Godfrey Weitzel. This became the first and only all-black army corps in American military history. By 20 October 1864, there were 140 black regiments in the Union army with a total strength of 101,950 men. Black troops were not confined to infantry and artillery units alone. By October 1864 there were also six black cavalry regiments in the Union army.[66]

Matched by the role of the black soldiers in the Virginia campaign was the work of the black soldiers farther south. On 15 August 1864, General Joseph Wheeler attacked the Union

forces at Dalton, Georgia. General James B. Steedman was
the Union commander of this district with headquarters at
Chattanooga. He dispatched Colonel James J. Morgan's
division, which contained the Fourteenth Black Infantry Regiment,
to Dalton. This was the Fourteenth Regiment's first action.
The black regiment held the left during the engagement.
General Steedman was anxious to know how these ex-slaves
would behave under fire, thus he ordered one of his aides to
observe the black regiment and report how it was fighting. The
aide reported that under the brave and competent officers of the
Fourteenth the battle lines were perfect and the firing regular
and effective. He further reported that he looked on with
amazement at these blacks, so recently from bondage, who
fought like veterans. When the battle was over and the
Fourteenth Regiment marched into Dalton, the white soldiers,
who were reluctant to fight with them at first, showered them
with praise. This was the first major action in which black
troops of the Army of the Cumberland had participated. Their
behavior at Dalton won the admiration and respect of the white
soldiers. Colonel Morgan reported later that words were
inadequate to describe the gallantry and impetuosity of the
black troops at Dalton. [67]

Having earned a reputation for steady and gallant fighting,
the Fourteenth was dispatched in pursuit of the routed and
decimated troops of General Wheeler through East and Middle
Tennessee. On the march and in camp the Fourteenth exhibited
the highest soldierly qualities and displayed enthusiasm that
their white comrades could not comprehend. The black soldier
was fighting to win a new dignity and self-respect, and for an
America in which his children would have greater liberties and
responsibilities. [68]

On 27 September 1864, the Fourteenth joined General Lovell
H. Rousseau, commander of a force of cavalry at Pulaski,
Tennessee, where it participated in action against the
Confederates under General Nathan B. Forrest. Rousseau had
been driven all day, and his cavalry was exhausted; but Forrest
met a steady and effective fire from the black infantry. After
testing the Union line and finding it unyielding, he recoiled,
turned to the east, and struck over toward Murfreesboro. This
was considered a great victory for the Fourteenth Division because
they had stood face to face with a triumphant force of Southern

cavalry and stopped their progress. They had done what
Rousseau's veterans could not do. Colonel Morgan and the
Fourteenth returned to Chattanooga after his battle and eagerly
awaited another assignment.[69]

One of the important engagements of 1864 was the Battle of
Nashville. In early December the Confederate Army of Tennessee,
consisting of about forty-four thousand men and commanded by
General John B. Hood, encamped on the outskirts of Nashville.
They prepared for an attack on the Union forces which General
William T. Sherman had left behind when he started his march
to the sea. The Army of the Cumberland, commanded by General
George H. Thomas, was ordered to take the initiative by
attacking the Confederate forces at Nashville. The brigades
selected by General Thomas for the opening attack consisted
almost entirely of blacks under the command of General James
B. Steedman. Black troops were exposed to severe fire from
close-range artillery during the battle. For two full days in
battle the black troops behaved with great courage. Hood's
veteran army was beaten and demoralized. Eight black regiments--
the Twelfth, Thirteenth, Fourteenth, Sixteenth, Seventeenth,
Eighteenth, Forty-fourth, and One Hundredth--played a vital role
in the Union victory. When this two-day encounter ended, one
of the Confederate armies was completely destroyed. General
Steedman, a prominent Breckinridge Democrat before the war,
was frank in his appreciation of the role of the black regiments.
He pointed out that most of his losses were black troops and
that the severe loss among the black troops was because of
their brilliant charge on the enemy's works on Overton Hill. He
further stated that he was unable to discover that color made
any difference in the fighting of his troops. All, white and
black, nobly did their duty as soldiers.[70]

Black soldiers won an enviable reputation by their stubborn
fighting with the Army of the Frontier under General James G.
Blunt, General John M. Schofield, and General Frederick Steele.
They battled repeatedly against General Nathan B. Forrest in
Tennessee and Mississippi. At Wolf River Bridge,
Tennessee, the Second Infantry Regiment of West Tennessee
was formally commended by its commander. Nine black regiments
participated in reducing Fort Blakely in the final assault on

Mobile. Black regiments also fought extensively in Florida, Georgia, South Carolina, and North Carolina during the last year of the war.[71]

In the final four months of the war, as William T. Sherman advanced in the Carolinas and Ulysses S. Grant hammered harder at Richmond, blacks continued to perform their duties well as soldiers. During the winter of 1864-65 twenty-five regiments of black troops were concentrated on the James River, confronting the Confederate capital. By this time the black troops had a reputation that was respected in both armies. On 23 March 1865, President Lincoln left Washington to review the black soldiers on the James River. According to George Williams, the review was one of the most magnificent military spectacles of the Civil War. Twenty-five thousand black soldiers, in bright new uniforms, well drilled, well armed, and well commanded, passed in review before the President, General Grant, and the general officers of the Armies of the James and Potomac. President Lincoln was deeply moved at the sight of these black troops, against whose employment he had earlier and earnestly protested. The entire review made a deep impression upon the thousands of white soldiers and military chiefs who witnessed it, and they were very vocal in their praise of the black comrades in arms.[72]

The prejudice against the employment of black troops among conservative members of Congress had almost disappeared by 1865. Moreover, there was now a movement in Congress to make amends for the bad treatment and neglect which black soldiers had suffered. Accordingly, on 31 January 1865, a constitutional amendment prohibiting slavery was proposed by Congress. The news of this action had salutary effect upon the black troops in the field. They had begun to see some of the rewards of their valor as soldiers.[73]

On 6 February 1865, General Robert E. Lee was appointed general-in-chief of the Confederate army. The Confederacy was almost a year behind the Union government in conferring unified command. Among the many new features which General Lee immediately sought to incorporate in his war policy was the military employment of blacks by the Confederate government. He had experienced the excellent fighting of black troops in the Union army and urged the military employment of blacks to help

53

save the Confederacy. On 20 February the Confederate House passed a bill authorizing the employment of blacks as soldiers, but the Senate promptly rejected the measure. The movement, however, finally received the approval of the Confederate government on 20 March 1865. Though a few black troops were recruited, none actually served in battle because the Confederate government's approval of the employment of black soldiers was passed on the eve of their surrender.[74]

By early 1865, the only operations that could have bearing upon the main outcome of the war were those in Virginia and the Carolinas. Only blind hope existed in the South at this time. President Davis made it known to President Lincoln on 12 January that he was willing to open negotiations if they would bring peace to both countries. But to Lincoln there was one country. Despite this disagreement, a conference was held on 3 February between Lincoln and Seward for the Union and Vice-President Alexander Stephens, R.M.T. Hunter, and John A. Campbell for the Confederacy. Various matters were discussed, but the conference adjourned without reaching an agreement. The major point of disagreement was Lincoln's insistence that the Confederate armies be disbanded. But the Confederacy still demanded independence as a nation before there could be peace.[75]

In the meantime, General Sherman continued his advancement through the Carolinas aiming for a junction with Grant in Virginia. On 17 February Columbia, the capital of South Carolina, was taken. Charleston, known to many as the birthplace of secession, was now completely cut off and occupied on the 18th without a fight. General Schofield took Wilmington, North Carolina, and on 22 February General Lee reinstated General Joseph E. Johnston. General Johnston was now assigned the task of stopping Sherman's advance through the Carolinas. Black soldiers contributed to the success of General Sherman's armies as they swept into Savannah and then northward. The first Union troops to march into the city of Charleston after its fall included the Twenty-first Black Infantry, followed soon afterward by detachments of the Fifty-fourth and Fifty-fifth Massachusetts Regiments.[76]

General Sherman encountered a problem as he advanced through the South that his meticulous planning had not foreseen. At every encampment flocks of blacks appeared. The coming of Sherman's army was spread by black runners traveling during the night from plantation to plantation. General Sherman informed them that they would slow down his line of march and drain his army of needed food and supplies. He further informed them that Union triumph on the battlefield would result in their freedom and insisted that they remain on the plantations. Some thirty-five thousand blacks ignored his advice. Why wait until the end of the war for freedom when they could have it right away by simply attaching themselves to the army? It was hard to turn them back as they begged to stay. But these blacks who joined Sherman were not confined to the receiving end. From the very beginning they gave incalculable assistance as Sherman astounded his foes by his ability to move some sixty-five thousand troops, loaded army wagons and heavy artillery at a pace averaging ten miles a day in spite of rain-sogged roads, flooded lowlands, dense swamps, swollen streams, and intersecting rivers.[77]

After a conference on 27-28 March on the River Queen in the James River at City Point with President Lincoln, General Sherman, Sheridan, Meade, and Ord, Grant launched his final offensive campaign. General Lee's long line in defense of Richmond was now so thinly manned that a break was inevitable, while Grant was strengthened by the arrival of General Sheridan, who had shifted his army southward from Winchester and joined the Army of the Potomac. The all-black Twenty-fifth Corps, under the command of General Godfrey Weitzel, was also moved to Richmond. In the last important battle of the war at Five Forks on 1 April, Lee's army was overwhelmed and vigorous assaults upon the Confederate lines covering Petersburg followed in which large numbers of Confederates were taken prisoners.[78]

On the following day, General Lee gave the order for the evacuation of Petersburg. It was now obvious that Petersburg was untenable and that Richmond would also fall. Union forces moved in and took possession of the city the next day. President Davis was attending services in St. Paul's Church in Richmond when he received news of the fall of Petersburg. With his cabinet and government, he quickly began preparation for leaving the capital city. It was now a matter of retreat and pursuit by Lee and Grant. In the closing campaign of the war, black soldiers continued to perform their duties well. Black troops of the Fifth Massachusetts Cavalry were the first soldiers to enter Richmond after its fall on 3 April, followed closely by the Twenty-fifth Army Corps, the all-black corps of thirty-two regiments. The fall of Richmond evoked rejoicing in the North, for the surrender of the Confederate capital clearly marked the deathblow to the Confederacy.[79]

General Lee managed his escape well, getting away with nearly all his artillery. Grant feared that Lee might escape into North Carolina and join General Johnston. Some of the most rapid movement of the war now occurred. Black troops performed bravely in all the conflicts, skirmishes, rear-guard actions, and sudden encounters at crossroads and bridges in which they participated during the closing weeks of the war. It does not come within the scope of this work to describe the movements and strategies of the Union and Confederate forces in this final action.

When the Confederacy had been defeated and the war was over, more than thirty black regiments (nearly all the Twenty-fifth Corps) were transferred to the Department of Texas for duty along the Rio Grande, to give force to State Department protests against French interference in Mexico.[80]

More than 186,000 black men served as soldiers in the Union army. They were crucial to the whole Union war effort. These men fought in 449 engagements, of which 39 were major battles. Approximately 37,300 black soldiers lost their lives while serving in the Union army. Seventeen black soldiers were awarded Congressional Medals of Honor. Testimony to the martial valor of black soldiers came from friends as well as enemies. They disappointed their enemies and surprised their friends. They exhibited the highest qualities of soldiership at Port Hudson, Milliken's Bend, Olustee, Chaffin's Farm, Fort Wagner, Moscow Bridge, and many other engagements too numerous to mention.[81]

To measure the contribution of the black soldier to Union victory in the Civil War involves more than counting Congressional Medals of Honor, casualties, and listing engagements. Actual combat takes a relatively small part of a soldiers's time and energy. By and large, black soldiers shared every kind of soldier's duty with their white comrades. They guarded prisoners, prepared fortifications, escorted wagon trains, paraded for visiting dignitaries, worked and drilled. Whatever duties they performed, black soldiers responded to the Union call when war weariness and anti-black feeling were at high tide in the North. Despite discrimination in pay and duty, and the constant threat of death or return to slavery if captured, black soldiers did not desert in abnormally large numbers.[82]

CHAPTER III

BLACK SAILORS IN THE UNION NAVY

While black soldiers were fighting creditably for Union survival on the battlefield, black sailors were also performing their duties effectively during battle action. The role of the Union navy in determining the outcome of the Civil War has long been recognized as decisive. Blacks constituted some twenty-five percent of the total naval personnel, they behaved well, occasionally with conspicuous gallantry under fire. Their contribution, particularly in terms of information concerning the enemy's potential, disposition, and terrain, was invaluable.

Unlike the army, the United States Navy did not follow a Jim Crow policy. Throughout its history, the navy had permitted free blacks to enlist. In the seventeenth century, blacks were widely employed on privateers, trading vessels, and fishing boats. Some of the most distinguished figures in black history during the eighteenth and nineteenth centuries earned their livelihoods, at some point in their careers, by a maritime occupation. Blacks were not uncommon in the Continental and state navies during the Revolutionary War, and they played a conspicuous part in the naval fighting of the War of 1812. Throughout the pre-Civil War period, maritime pursuits formed one of the most important types of employment for blacks.[1]

When the Civil War started there were many free blacks in the navy, and in September 1861 the navy adopted a policy of enlisting former slaves. Because of a shortage of men during the entire war, the navy encouraged the blacks to join. They responded well and eventually 29,511 joined the Union fleet. In addition to the fact that blacks traditionally had followed the sea, other forces led many to join the navy during the Civil War. Since blacks were not allowed to enlist in the Union army until the latter part of 1862, the navy was the only way that they could get involved in the war. Secondly, from the very beginning of the war, fugitive slaves flocked in large numbers to Union vessels after their services were refused by the Union army. Commanding naval officers informed Secretary of Navy Gideon Welles of this action and suggested that the blacks be employed. Secretary Welles replied that, while it was not the policy of the government to invite or encourage slave desertions, yet under the circumstances there was no other course to take without violating every principle of humanity. To return the fugitives would be impolitic as well as cruel.[2]

Blacks continued to flock to the Union vessels in large numbers. On 25 September 1861, the Secretary of Navy declared that his department had found it necessary to adopt a regulation with respect to the large and increasing number of blacks who had entered the navy yards and boarded Union ships. Welles stated that the blacks could neither be expelled from the service to which they had resorted, nor could they be maintained unemployed, but it was not proper that they should be compelled to render necessary and regular services without a stated compensation. He, therefore, authorized the enlistment of fugitives when their services could be made useful. They would be enlisted in the navy under the same forms and regulation as the other enlistments. Secretary Welles further stated, however, that the fugitives would not be allowed higher ratings than a boy or apprentice (this was amended in December 1862) at a compensation of ten dollars per month and one ration a day.[3]

The conditions in the navy were more attractive to the blacks than those in the army. In October 1861, the Army of the Department of Virginia ordered that all contrabands employed as servants by officers or others would receive eight dollars per month (four dollars for women), and that all other blacks under the protection of the troops, not employed as servants, would be immediately put to work, in either the engineer's or quartermaster's departments. Boys from twelve to eighteen would receive five dollars per month and able-bodied men ten dollars plus rations. The former received only one dollar a month in actual cash, the latter two dollars, while the remainder went to the departments to pay for clothing and to help support women, children, and the disabled. It is understandable why a considerable number of blacks served in the navy, where they received ten dollars a month, were entitled to all privileges on the ship, and had absolute control of their earnings. This was a strong incentive for them to prefer the sea to the land service, when the latter only realized two dollars per month. Another incentive for fugitive slaves to serve in the Union navy was the fact that they were liable for very harsh treatment if captured. But it was very rare for a Union ship to be captured by the Confederacy.[4]

60

Throughout the war the navy suffered from a chronic and serious shortage of manpower because of several factors in addition to the enormous expansion from a total of 76 vessels in March 1860 to 671 vessels in December 1861. From 1861 to 1865 a total of 1,059 vessels were commissioned by the navy. Enlistment in the navy, unlike that in the army, carried no bounty payment. The draft also made men subject to the army, but not the navy. Servicemen in the navy were not credited to their community or state draft quotas, which created a serious inhibition against enlistment in the navy. Since blacks did not receive bounties for army enlistment and were not subject to the draft until the latter part of the war, these regulations adversely affected the willingness of whites to join the navy but had no effect on the blacks. These conditions, therefore, forced the navy to encourage the enlistment of blacks, and probably accounted partially for the relatively favorable conditions under which the blacks served. Anxious to attract black recruits and to have them re-enlist when their terms expired, the navy tended to treat them fairly well. [5]

Because of an urgent request, the army turned over a considerable number of blacks to the navy. As early as the summer of 1862, Secretary of War Edwin Stanton ordered General John A. Dix at Fortress Monroe to turn over to the navy such contrabands as he may select for naval service. Twice during the month of January 1863, Secretary Welles appealed to Secretary Stanton to let him have up to four thousand fugitive slaves. Considerable numbers were transferred thereafter from the army to the navy. In addition, the navy made what was called enlistment landings in which naval officers went ashore and enlisted contrabands. [6]

Segregation and discrimination were at a minimum in the navy. Blacks were messed and quartered in common with other sailors, many were frequently of superior rank to fellow white crewmen. However, with the enlistment of thousands of fugitive slaves a certain amount of discriminatory practice prevailed, but much less than that which generally prevailed in the civil society and army during this period. Regulations closed certain positions to blacks, but they were not strictly enforced. Contrabands were often employed in tasks normally required of men having a higher rating than that accorded them. The use of contrabands as pilots was commonly practiced. In 1863 Admiral Samuel F. DuPont wrote to Secretary Welles informing him that he had added some contraband pilots and authorized payment at thirty to forty dollars per month. He further stated that the blacks were skillful and competent. Blacks were, however, used in disproportionate numbers in unhealthy and dangerous work. Some of the white officers were more prejudiced than others toward the blacks. Some believed that blacks could perform better than whites in the hot southern sun and were less prone to diseases; therefore, only blacks were used under certain conditions.[7]

Battle casualty statements reveal that blacks were killed, captured and wounded in action aboard at least forty-nine different naval vessels. The first recorded black naval casualties were the deaths, in action, of Robert McKinsey and Robert Willinger on 31 January 1862, aboard the Keystone State near Charleston, South Carolina, while the last were the deaths in action of G. D. Andrew and James Glen, aboard the Althea in Mobile Bay, Alabama, on 12 April 1865. It is estimated that about three thousand Union black sailors died from disease and enemy action during the war.[8]

Blacks held all ranks in the navy except petty officer. The technical position of pilot, in many respects, was equivalent to that of a commissioned officer. Blacks were particularly numerous aboard gunboats. A few Union vessels were manned by a predominantly black crew. The gunboat Glide, lost at Cairo in February 1863, was reported to have had a crew of thirty-eight of which thirty were contrabands. When Stepping Stones conducted operation in Mattox Creek, Virginia, in March 1865, only two of its crew of thirty were white. Fifteen black sailors of various ratings served on the Union vessel Kearsarge during the engagement with the daring Confederate Alabama. In this historic duel in which the famed Alabama went down, Joachim Pease, a black crewman on the Kearsarge, won the Congressional Medal of Honor.[9]

The unique and inestimable value of the black sailor to the Union navy was his acquaintance with the enemy and the terrain. Information as to the location, strength, disposition, movements and activities of the enemy, both of land and naval forces, was supplied by blacks to all echelons of the Union command. It is impossible to study the thousands of firsthand reports from naval officers without concluding that the greatest single source of military and naval intelligence, particularly on a tactical level, for the Union government was the black man. Considering the crucial importance of information concerning the enemy for any successful military operation, it may be asserted that these thousands of willing eager scouts, spies, guides, pilots, and informers, available only to the Union forces, constituted a major source of superiority for the Union forces as opposed to their enemy.[10]

Blacks, both enlisted and civilian, also provided the Union navy with information making possible the destruction or capture of valuable stores of sugar, rice, cotton, corn and salt, as well as for the destruction or capture of entire vessels. On 5 January 1865, a fugitive slave came to the Winnebago, in Mobile Bay, and informed its commander of the location of several enemy sloops and valuable stores, without armed guards. The commander promptly dispatched an expedition which returned with four captured vessels and much material, and reported they met no opposition.[11]

Favorable comments on the behavior of individuals or groups of blacks are numerous. Reporting on a successful raid upon a Confederate steamer in Suwanee River, South Carolina, on 25 March 1864, Commander A. W. Weaver praised the conduct of five black sailors who had behaved admirably under fire. Another daring adventure in November 1862, culminating in the kidnapping of a postman with much official mail destined for Charleston, South Carolina, was accomplished by a white petty officer and three unnamed enlisted contrabands. A fierce hand-to-hand encounter that marked the surprise boarding and subsequent capture of the USS Water Witch in Ossabaw Sound, South Carolina, in June 1864, left only one Union survivor. This lone survivor was a contraband named Peter McIntosh who managed to escape. According to the report of Admiral J. A. Dahlgren to the Secretary of the Navy, it was his escape and the warnings he then gave that saved several other Union vessels.[12]

Of the thousands of slaves who escaped and came into the Union navy the most spectacular was Robert Smalls and his party. Unparalleled for audacity, Small's feat was carefully planned and brilliantly executed. Robert Smalls was born in Beaufort County, South Carolina, in 1839, the son of a Jewish father and a black mother. His father was a sailmaker and rigger of schooners, sloops, and other ships, and Smalls learned the sailmaker's trade at an early age and later became a master rigger. He helped his father in delivering boats to their owners on plantations and in towns and large cities, and from experience he gained valuable knowledge of the shoals and currents of the waters in the Charleston area. When Fort Sumter was fired on April 1861, Smalls was pressed into the Confederate service and installed as pilot on the Confederate transport, the Planter, with a black crew under him and two white officers as his superiors. He successfully persuaded the black crew to flee with him in the hope of becoming free. On the night of 12 May 1862, the white officers in control of the Planter spent the night in the city of Charleston, as was their habit once or twice a week, for recreation. Shortly after the white officers had departed, Smalls and his crew placed their families and belongings on the boat and early the next morning started out of the harbor with the seized Planter.[13]

Smalls delivered the Planter to the Union navy and said, "I thought the Planter might be of some use to Uncle Abe." The Planter was a three hundred ton, side-wheel, wood-burning, armed steamer. At the time it was heavily loaded with munitions of war, food, and other supplies. So spectacular was Smalls's exploit that the commanding officer sent a full report to the Secretary of the Navy and recommended that Smalls and his associates be given prize money for the Planter. With unusual speed, the Senate passed a bill authorizing the Secretary of the Navy to have the Planter appraised and gave one-half of the appraised value to Smalls and the other members of his crew. Within a month, the House passed the measure and President Lincoln signed it. Smalls and his crew were also invited to Washington to meet President Lincoln.[14]

More important to the naval command than the guns and other supplies of the Planter was Smalls's intimate knowledge of the intricacies of the Sea Island coastal waters. The information furnished by Smalls was so noteworthy that the Secretary of the Navy, in his annual report to President Lincoln, stated that it made possible the capture of Stono. The seizure of Stono Inlet and river secured an important base for military operations. Smalls served as pilot of the Planter and other vessels operating along the South Carolina coastline during the rest of the war. Many southern blacks served as pilots along the South Carolina and Georgia coastline because navigating these sinuous channels required the skill and knowledge that came only from years of experience.[15]

64

Nine Union ironclads under Flag Officer Samuel DuPont went into Charleston Harbor and attacked Fort Sumter on 7 April 1863, about a year after Smalls had escaped to freedom. The Keokuk, one of the Union's ironclads, was struck ninety-five times before it sank to the bottom. During the battle, Smalls enjoyed a distinction that had never been bestowed upon a black American-- that of being one of the pilots during the fight. He remained at this post during the battle until the ship went down. When the Union flag was again raised over Fort Sumter in April 1865, the Planter, with Smalls as pilot, brought more than two thousand blacks to the ceremony.[16]

William Tillman, a black man, performed another spectacular naval exploit and became one of the first authentic northern war heroes. He was a steward and cook aboard the schooner S. J. Waring. The S. J. Waring was a vessel of three hundred tons bound in early July 1861 for South America from New York with an assorted cargo. The schooner was captured on 7 July by the daring Confederate privateer, Jeff Davis. The captured Waring was declared a prize of the Confederate States of America. Its captain and four of the crew members were taken aboard the privateer with only three of the original crew remaining on the Waring. One of those remaining was the strongly built twenty-seven year old William Tillman. In place of the five men who were removed, the Jeff Davis substituted a crew of five men and set sail for the port of Charleston, South Carolina. Tillman was told that he was henceforth the property of the Confederate States and would be sold on arrival at Charleston as a slave.[17]

The ship was within a hundred miles of the port when Tillman decided to carry out a plan of action he had devised. On 16 July near midnight, while three of the crew members were sleeping, Tillman killed them with a hatchet and threw them overboard. He forced the remaining two members to take orders from him, proclaiming himself master of the vessel. With the assistance of the original two crew members, Tillman headed toward New York with the stars and stripes flying proudly. The Waring arrived at New York on Sunday, 21 July, and Tillman was immediately showered with praise. Tillman had left New York as a steward and cook, but returned as captain of the ship. The ship and its cargo were valued at over one hundred thousand dollars. The Federal Government later awarded Tillman the sum of six thousand dollars as prize money for the capture of the vessel.[18]

Before the excitement over the Waring incident had died down, another black seaman was making the news. His name was Jacob Garrick, a twenty-five year old steward of the Enchantress. On 29 June 1861, the Enchantress left Boston enroute to Cuba with an assorted cargo. It was also seized by the Confederate Jeff Davis on 22 July, shortly after the capture of the Waring. The entire crew of the Enchantress, except Garrick, was removed. A prize crew took over the ship and set sail for Charleston. The captain of the prize crew had taken the precaution of providing himself with clearance papers for the Enchantress, with the intention of representing his crew as the original crew if stopped by a Union war ship. Later that day, the U.S.S. Albatross, of the Atlantic Blockading Squadron, stopped the Enchantress. As the Albatross approached and the crew of the Enchantress was questioned, Garrick jumped overboard shouting that the vessel had been captured by the Jeff Davis and was enroute to Charleston. Jacob Garrick was responsible for saving the Enchantress.[19]

Another spectacular naval exploit was performed by Mary Louvestre, a trusted slave. She overheard conversations between her master, who was an engineer, and other high ranking Confederate engineers concerning the remodeling of the Merrimac. One engineer stated that within a few months the Confederacy would have a naval monster that would blow Abe Lincoln's navy right out of the water. Carrying food to her master, Simeon Louvestre, the next day at the Norfolk Navy Yard, she entered the chief engineer's office and saw the secret designs for the ironclad Merrimac, now renamed the Virginia. Early the next morning before anyone arrived at the navy yard, Mary went to the chief engineer's office and copied the secret designs. As an expert seamstress, she traced the drawings of the Virginia accurately.[20]

Later in the week, Mary asked her master if she could have permission to visit her previous old master and mistress in the valley. Having implicit faith in Mary, Simeon Louvestre gave her a note stating that she was traveling with his permission. Traveling by day and night, she later arrived outside Fredericksburg and was directed by a black teamster to the headquarters of the Union Lodge, a secret organization for aiding escaped slaves and Union spies. There she obtained a guide who led her through the lines to Centerville on the Union side. Taking the design all the way to Washington, she accepted congratulations from

Secretary Welles for brave and quick-witted action. He offered her freedom and a job, but she preferred to return home and await freedom there. As a voluntary Union spy, she hastened the completion of the Monitor and the Union navy was not destroyed. Mary Louvestre remains an unsung heroine in American history.[21]

The Union navy had its list of unsung blacks who discharged their duties effectively during battle action, but who did nothing spectacular to win official commendation. Blacks were aboard the Monitor in its famed engagement with the Merrimac or Virginia. Black sailors fulfilled a variety of roles in the Union navy. They served on vessels engaged in coastal blockades and also hunted down enemy privateers. On the docks, black men were equally active as laborers unloading supplies and equipment.[22]

Four black members of the Union navy, however, behave with such outstanding gallantry that they received the nation's most coveted award, the Congressional Medal of Honor. Aaron Anderson, landsman on the Wyandank, was awarded the Medal of Honor for bravery while serving with an expedition on Mattox Creek, Virginia, 16-18 March 1865. He participated with a boat crew in the clearing of Mattox Creek. Anderson carried out his duties courageously in the face of opposing fire which cut away half the oars, pierced the launch in many places, and cut the barrel off a musket being fired at the enemy.

A second black sailor to win the Congressional Medal of Honor was Robert Blake, listed only as "contraband" who was a crew member of the Marblehead. He enlisted in the navy after escaping from a Virginia plantation. In a bitter engagement with Confederate batteries on Stono River, South Carolina, 25 December 1863, Blake, serving as a powder boy, displayed extraordinary courage, alacrity, and intelligence in the discharge of his duty under trying circumstances.[22]

John Lawson, landsman aboard the flagship Hartford, in the battle of Mobile Bay, Alabama, 5 August 1864, earned the Medal of Honor for displaying outstanding valor. Lawson was one of six men stationed at the shell-whip on the berth deck who were killed or wounded by an enemy shell. Lawson was wounded in the leg and thrown violently against the side of the ship. Upon regaining his composure, he promptly returned to his station, although he was urged to go below for treatment of serious wounds. Lawson continued his duties throughout the remainder of the action.[24]

The fourth black sailor to win the Medal of Honor was Joachim Pease. He was awarded the Medal of Honor for gallantry under fire while serving aboard the Kearsarge on 19 June 1864. Acting as loader on the number two gun during the bitter engagement against the Confederate raider Alabama, off Cherbourg, France, Pease exhibited marked coolness and good conduct and was highly praised by his superior officer for gallantry under fire. In this historic encounter the Alabama was destroyed.[25]

Some black mariners fought on land as well as on sea. The naval campaign during the Civil War was unlike that of any other naval campaign in history, because it was fought largely in inland waters. Many times sailors were ordered ashore to conduct raids for food and supplies. Black sailors were crucial to the whole Union war effort.

While more than two hundred thousand black Americans in uniform were performing their duties creditably on the battlefield and seacoast, black civilians were not neglectful of home-front responsibilities. They also performed their duties creditably.

CHAPTER IV

BLACKS BEHIND THE LINES

Black civilians (North and South) made many noteworthy contributions to the Union war effort. Many black women worked in hospitals and camps as nurses, aides, and teachers. Many raised money for the families of the men at the front, worked with convalescent soldiers, and established and worked with relief agencies for ex-slaves. Thousands of slaves who came within Union lines worked as laborers, cooks, servants, spies, scouts, and guides. Northern black orators and writers were leaders in the struggle for emancipation and equal rights for blacks. They were leaders in the struggle for acceptance of black soldiers in the Union army as well as equal treatment after enlistment. Blacks were also very instrumental in the struggle for education and later suffrage for both the southern and northern blacks.

The Union spy system relied heavily upon information supplied by former slaves. Allan Pinkerton, founder and chief of the National Secret Service, stated that he found the blacks of invaluable assistance from the very beginning of the war. As chief of the National Detective Agency, all refugees, deserters, and contrabands who came into the lines of the Army of the Potomac were turned over to him for a thorough examination and for such future disposition as he recommended. After the examinations, Pinkerton would compile his findings and submit this information to the commanding general at the end of the day. Northern generals frequently obtained information on the location and size of enemy forces from contrabands who had entered Union lines. General Abner Doubleday, commander of the military defenses north of the Potomac, ordered that fugitive slaves should be encouraged to enter Union lines because they brought much valuable information which could not be obtained from any other source.[1]

John Scobell, a former Mississippi slave, became one of Allan Pinkerton's most trusted agents for the Army of the Potomac. When Scobell first came into the lines he appeared before Pinkerton for the customary questioning. Pinkerton was very impressed with Scobell's alert and straightforward answers to many of his questions. He also gave an intelligent account of his travels through the country, and was well informed as to the localities through which he had passed. Scobell gave such a detailed and knowledgeable account of his travels and of what he had seen that Pinkerton decided immediately to use him as a spy. Pinkerton states that for two weeks he employed Scobell in various capacities of minor importance, but those in which secrecy and loyalty were essential qualifications. His performance of these duties was all that could be desired. After the trial and training period, Pinkerton sent Scobell to several cities of Virginia with Timothy Webster to test his ability for active duty; his performance was superb.[2]

Scobell was a remarkably gifted man. He could sing and dance, as well as read and write. He worked as a cook, laborer, peddler, and entertainer on some of his missions. Repeatedly he went into Confederate territory, sometimes alone, to secure military information. On one occasion he made a trip into five towns in Confederate-held Virginia which took two weeks. Scobell also worked with Mrs. Hattie Lawton on several missions. Young and beautiful, no one suspected her of being a spy. Lawton posed as a lady of leisure and Scobell as her faithful servant. From these spies, Pinkerton secured valuable information which he submitted to the military high command. Scobell, therefore, deserves a place on the honor roll of the Civil War spies for his daring missions and for his services.[3]

George Scott, a contraband, set in motion one of the early battles of the Civil War. He was one of the earliest arrivals at Fortress Monroe, escaping from a plantation near Yorktown in May 1861. On the way to Fortress Monroe, he observed that the Confederates were entrenched at two points between Yorktown and Fortress Monroe. After his arrival at the fortress, Scott reported this information to Major Theodore Winthrop, the officer in charge. Winthrop discovered this report was accurate when Scott led him to these positions. As a result, Winthrop became convinced that the Confederates were planning a surprise attack designed to seize Newport and Hampton. Such a move, if successful, would isolate Fortress Monroe. Winthrop reported his findings and opinions to General Benjamin Butler, the commanding general. Butler decided to strike the first blow at Big Bethel, but he was unable to force the Confederate troops from these locations. However, it is noteworthy that a contraband played a significant role at this early date.

Henry Blake, another ex-slave, furnished valuable information to the command of General Don C. Buell in Kentucky. Blake spent his nights spying on Confederate positions and reporting his findings to Union officials the next day. On one occasion Blake, after learning from a slave girl that her master planned to meet with one of General Braxton Bragg's lieutenants, concealed himself in the room and overheard the discussion of plans. This information he sent to the Union officials. When Blake's activities became known, the Confederates offered a reward of one thousand dollars for him.[4]

Mrs. Elizabeth Van Lew, daughter of a very prominent Richmond family, became the best Union spy inside the Confederate capital. Defying old friends, and the civil and military authorities, she opposed slavery and the war. Throughout the war she was a dedicated and resourceful spy for the Union. After the victorious Union army arrived in Richmond, one of General Ulysses S. Grant's first visits was to her home.

Among the slaves Van Lew had freed was Mary Elizabeth Bowser. Mrs. Van Lew managed to get Bowser employed as a house servant of President Jefferson Davis. Mrs. Bowser was very intelligent and became an efficient spy in the Confederate President's home. She and her former mistress met at intervals after dark near the Van Lew farm. Bowser reported interesting stories and vital information to Mrs. Van Lew which she passed on to Union officials.[5]

Like many commanders, General George B. McClellan's indebtedness to blacks was great for the information he received from runaways and spies. Though he first rejected the runaways, he later realized that a slave might bring information that could save a whole army. Some of the most valuable information McClellan secured in regard to the position, movement and plans of the enemy, the topography of the country, and the inclination of certain inhabitants was obtained from contrabands.[6] General O. M. Mitchel, commander of the Union forces occupying north Alabama, reported to Secretary of War Edwin Stanton in 1862 on the importance of information obtained from contrabands and of his plan to employ slaves on the plantations as spies.[7]

Harriet Tubman, the renowned underground railroad operator of the antebellum years, worked as a spy and scout. During the decade of the fifties, Tubman had made nineteen trips into the South bringing out over three hundred slaves worth over a quarter of a million dollars. She was never captured nor did she lose a single "passenger." No other person was so successful in liberating slaves. By the end of the 1850s the slave owners of Maryland had posted rewards totaling forty thousand dollars for the arrest of the woman known to the slaves as "Moses." Because she was familiar with the South, she led Union raids deep into Confederate territory shortly after the war started. As a spy she appraised military and naval defenses of the South and reported on the location and quantity of supplies. She was well known and respected throughout the Union lines. General Rufus Saxton and other Union generals praised her for the many raids she led inside the enemy's lines in which she displayed remarkable courage and skill. Some of the generals used her both as a scout and as a liaison between the military officers and slaves in the raided regions.[8]

Disguised as an old hobbling black woman, Tubman could travel the inland roads of the South without being suspected as a Union spy. Not only did she gather information about troop movements, population, sources of supplies, and positions of artillery but she also formulated the strategy for guerilla raids into enemy territory to promote Union control over the slaves. Many of Mrs. Tubman's excursions into enemy territory were made in company with soldier details from Colonel James Montgomery's black brigade, the Second South Carolina volunteers. There were many daring and successful forays into the South Carolina interior, but none was more famous than the one up the Combahee River in which Mrs. Tubman and her troops surprised two Confederate encampments and freed over eight hundred slaves. Such raids were devastating to the morale of white southerners, emphasizing their vulnerability to Union forces even in the deep South. Tubman served in South Carolina from May 1862 until the end of the war. When the war ended in 1865, she was working as a nurse or matron in a military hospital. She received little monetary reward for her accomplishments. During her three years of service in South Carolina, she received only two hundred dollars from the government. However, in 1897 Congress granted her a twenty dollar monthly pension.[9]

One contraband who entered the Union lines in Virginia on 3 May 1863 and created much excitement was William A. Jackson, President Jefferson Davis's coachman. High ranking Union officers flocked around him. General Irvin McDowell, the commanding officer, immediately sent for him and telegraphed information he secured to Washington. Because Jackson could read and write and was very alert, he could give the Union military officials valuable information. He revealed the plans and campaign strategies he had overheard from President Davis and his subordinates, as well as the dissension that existed between the President and some of his generals.[10]

The Civil War, a spy-conscious war, saw more espionage, involving more people, than any in our history. The nature of the war made espionage easy to carry on and difficult to stop. At the war's beginning neither Union nor Confederacy had a security organization nor a secret service; the nation had never known one. Organized intelligence, however, gradually emerged in the two capitals and blacks played a decisive role. The complete story of American espionage from 1861-65 will never be known. Much of it was never committed to paper. Nevertheless, a great deal of data is available. In the Official Records of both armies are hundred of pages of correspondence dealing with espionage activities. The blacks of the South were acquainted with the roads, paths, fords, and other natural features of the country; thus, they made excellent guides, scouts, and spies. Un-questionably the contrabands constituted a potent military and naval resource for the Union. They demonstrated as spies, scouts, and guides that they would run great risks to serve the Union cause.[11]

Another very important contribution of blacks to the Union cause was their labor. During the war there were more than two hundred thousand black civilians in the service of the Union armies as laborers. By the end of the summer of 1862, the Union army had come to recognize the futility of its hands-off policy toward blacks and decided to hire and utilize fully their labor. Black labor was indispensable in every department. On 30 March 1862, General Ambrose Burnside appointed Vincent Coyler as Superintendent of the Poor for the Department of North Carolina, and authorized him to employ five thousand black laborers. In the Department of Tennessee, the labor of thousands of contrabands was supervised by John Eaton. The commanding officer of the Army of the Mississippi, General William S. Rosecrans, also made effective military use of contrabands.[12]

Blacks performed a variety of duties as laborers. According to Bobby L. Lovett, some seventy-two hundred laborers in Tennessee worked on the completion of the Northwestern Railroad which had been started by Confederates. The railroad ran seventy-five miles from Nashville to Johnsonville, Tennessee. This project was completed in the fall of 1863, in time for General William T. Sherman to gather and transport tons of supplies for his Atlanta campaign that began on 5 May 1864. Thousands were employed as woodchoppers, blacksmiths, gravediggers, teamsters, loaders and unloaders of supplies, bridge and road builders, constructors of hospital cots, as well as performing many other duties. Blacks were also excellent foragers. The Union armies, fighting and marching in enemy territory, frequently found it necessary to supply their food from the countryside.[13]

Blacks played a very decisive role in assisting General Sherman in his "march to the sea." On the second day, Sherman dispatched Major James C. McCoy to find black residents to question about the roads and bridges in the area. Sherman emphasized that he wanted black men questioned, not white men. Blacks served as pilots all along Sherman's march. Black assistance to the foragers was also incalculable. One of the notable features of the march was the skill and success of Sherman's army in rounding up mules, horses, cattle, poultry, hams, bags of corn meal and flour, sacks of potatoes, and other provisions. Blacks helped locate these supplies, exhuming them from pits and cellars, as well as getting them from barns, granaries, smokehouses, and gardens. Once the supplies were found, the former slaves aided in transporting them. Sherman's success in feeding over sixty-five thousand troops while on the march in enemy country was one of the most remarkable feats in history; without the help of the blacks this would have been impossible. These black laborers were among the troops who lifted the bulky army wagons and cannons from the mudholes, helped construct bridges, and repaired roads.

Sherman also used blacks in tearing down as well as building up. A believer in total war, he made it a point to destroy anything of possible value to the enemy. Blacks helped in the destruction of railroads, depots, mills, factories, machine shops, stores, and everything else of military value. These black laborers, servants, and teamsters also provided appreciated entertainment for the soldiers at night.[14]

Throughout the war southern blacks rendered valuable assistance to northern soldiers who escaped from Confederate prisons and were trying to find their way back to Union lines. Many prisoners stated that it would have been impossible for them to have reached Union lines without the aid of the blacks who were in a position to give marked assistance. A long familiarity with the operations of the underground railroad had given them valuable experience in the techniques of flight concealment. The slaves knew the bypaths and short cuts in the woods, the location of the patrol guard's nightly beat, and the position of the Confederate pickets. They were able to ascertain whether cavalry scouts were in the vicinity searching for escaped soldiers. They also furnished information on the location of whites who secretly sympathized with the Union cause. The prison literature of the Civil War is full of stories about slaves and the slave guides who helped escaping Union soldiers.[15]

Black women and men behind the lines also contributed to the war effort by serving as nurses and aides in caring for the sick and wounded. With the firing on Fort Sumter the position of women in America underwent a change. Dr. Elizabeth Blackwell, the first woman in the world to be awarded a doctoral degree in medicine, believed that the deplorable nursing situation must be improved. The Union military hospitals at the beginning of the war were small. The largest contained only forty beds. No trained and efficient medical staff was provided. There were no female nurses, and the few male nurses were poorly trained. At many hospitals, patients were cared for by poorly paid and generally incompetent attendants. In some cities, law violators were sentenced by the court to work in these hospitals providing nursing care for the patients.

On 29 April 1861, Dr. Blackwell called a meeting of the leading women of New York to plan for some kind of nursing care to meet the emergency. The Women's Central Relief Association of New York was organized and Dr. Blackwell outlined the required qualifications for a nurse. Within a few weeks the association had chosen, from hundreds of candidates, one hundred competent women to be trained as nurses for three months.[16]

Church groups, private charity groups, and prominent individuals also established programs to train nurses to be sent to the front. Some of these women were trained by serving short terms of apprenticeship in available hospitals throughout the country. On June 1861, the Secretary of War issued an order creating the United States Sanitary Commission, a forerunner of the American Red Cross. Among its many duties, the Commission investigated conditions in army hospitals and camps; supplied nurses and matrons to hospitals; studied problems of sanitation and general hygiene; supplied food, clothing, and medicine to the troops. The Commission also introduced hospital cars for the human transportation of the wounded. As women, both black and white, volunteered in increasing numbers, Secretary of War Simon Cameron appointed Dorothea Dix as Superintendent of Nurses. According to Aloysius Plaisance and Leo F. Schelver, III, the Union military hospitals in Nashville by May and June of 1863 were operating in an efficient manner. To care for the casualties from battles fought near Nashville, the Union army took over many buildings and converted them into military hospitals. The staff in these hospitals consisted of male and female nurses, both black and white. Blacks also served as cooks, aides, servants, and laundresses.[17]

Harriet Tubman, previously mentioned, was also a respected nurse in the Department of the South. Thousands of the slaves on the South Carolina Sea Islands were suffering from a wide range of diseases. In caring for the sick and wounded, Tubman's influence was unique, as the slaves believed she possessed great powers of healing. From her mother she had learned much about the healing properties of herbs, and she gained a great reputation as a healer. A tea that she used for treating yellow fever became famous.[18]

Another black woman who served the Union cause as a nurse in the Sea Islands was Susie King Taylor, a former Georgia slave and the wife of a sergeant in the First South Carolina Volunteers, later the Thirty-third United States Colored Infantry. She was employed as a company laundress, but she also served as a nurse and teacher. As a volunteer nurse, Mrs. Taylor gave her services in the badly understaffed hospitals in the Sea Islands.[19]

Sojourner Truth was another well known black women who served as a nurse in the Union camps and hospitals. She was born a slave in 1797 in Ulster County, New York. Her master named her Isabella Baumfree. She and her brothers and sisters were later sold to a New York farmer. Although slavery was ended by law in New York, her master did not free her until 1827. She became deeply religious and devoted her life to the abolition of slavery and equal rights for blacks and women. She also changed her name to Sojourner Truth, stating that the Lord gave her this new name meaning that her mission was to travel and preach the truth. She also distributed gifts to the soldiers and entertained them by singing spirituals, many of her own compositions.

However, this legendary lady confined her work to the camps in the North because she was too old to go to southern camps. In 1864, she met with President Lincoln and remained in Washington for over a year working in the Freedmen's Village at Arlington Heights.[20]

Nurses and missionaries, both black and white, served also in contraband camps. Disloyal slaves ran away from their masters in a quest for personal freedom after the war started, but freedom all to often led them to the torments of poverty. Slaves owned little or no property and in leaving their owners they forsook a guaranteed subsistence. Unless they had stolen some of their masters' property, the contrabands had no significant resources beyond their ability to work. Many freedmen admitted that they had greater material advantages while in slavery.

Life in these contraband camps were not easy. Many contrabands died from diseases and exposure. Some camps had a death rate of twenty-five percent. Most of those who died were women and children as they made up the greatest percentage of inhabitants. From 1862 to 1865 more deaths occurred from colds and diseases caused by exposure to severe weather than from any other cause. The quality of contraband camp housing varied widely. Most camps began with tents or vacant buildings. Often the tents were so worn that they provided little actual shelter from weather. Lack of adequate food, medical supplies, and clothing also contributed to the high death rate in these camps. According to John Vincent Cimprich, Jr., the death toll during the winter of 1862-63 alone ran as high as twelve hundred in Memphis and fourteen hundred in Nashville. Yet, despite these problems, most contrabands preferred to remain in these camps rather than return to slavery.[21]

Blacks were active in the organization of schools for freedmen. Southern state laws had made it a crime to teach blacks to read and write. The first contraband school in the South was started by Mary Chase, a freedwoman of Alexandria, Virginia, on 1 September 1861. In subsequent months, Alexandria blacks established several schools for the freedmen. Missionary associations, both black and white, as well as individuals were very instrumental in establishing schools for the freedmen. The African Civilization Society of New York, which had been founded in 1858 to promote American black missionary effort and settlement in Africa, reconstituted itself during the Civil War as a freedmen's aid society. The society established six schools in Washington for the freedmen. In addition, twenty-two blacks individually started private schools for contrabands in Washington. Northern black churches also established schools for the freedmen throughout the South. Black women in Natchez, Mississippi, established three schools during the war. In Savannah, blacks could boast not only of two large schools which they had founded but also of a black board of education to determine the policies.[22]

The most prominent of the philanthropic organizations to establish schools in the South for blacks during the war was the American Missionary Association (AMA). Lewis Tappan, treasurer of the AMA, wrote General Benjamin Butler, commander of the Department of Virginia, in August 1861 and offered association services. Butler welcomed their services, and the Reverend Charles Lockwood found the blacks in a state of poverty beyond which he had imagined. However, he found that they were willing to help themselves as far as possible and that they realized their primary need was education. Hence, Lockwood obtained permission not only to teach the contrabands to read but also to bring as many teachers as he thought necessary to achieve this purpose. Thus, from the very outset, the mission of the AMA in regard to the contrabands was to have a threefold nature: to promote their physical well-being, to contribute to their intellectual improvement, and to work for their spiritual welfare.[23]

On 15 September 1861, Lockwood opened a Sunday School for blacks in the home of former President John Tyler, who had abandoned his home and left for Richmond, and two days later the first day school opened with Mary S. Peake as the teacher. Mrs. Peake, daughter of a black free mother and white father, was born in Norfolk, Virginia, in 1823. She grew up in Alexandria and received a good education. As a young woman before the war, she had taught many blacks to read. Blacks had come to her cabin at night in large numbers to receive her instruction.

Mrs. Peake had twenty students in her school on the first day of its operation at Hampton, Virginia, but within a week the number had grown to fifty. She taught children from nine o'clock until noon and held classes for adults in the afternoon. Her curriculum included spelling, reading, writing, elements of arithmetic, and religious lessons. Within a few months the AMA had established several more schools in Hampton, as well as schools for blacks in Norfolk, Portsmouth, Newport News, and on several plantations. By 1864 more than three thousand blacks were attending school in the Department of Virginia with fifty-two teachers; at least five of the teachers were black. The teachers were paid by the association, but the government furnished them with subsistence. Mrs. Peake's teaching career was short as she died in March 1862. With her death, Mary Peake became an inspiration to the cause of teaching and helping these illiterate blacks. The people and organizations responsible for establishing these schools—northerners and southerners, whites and blacks—made a most significant contribution to the adjustment of blacks coming out of slavery.[24]

One aspect of the Civil War which has not received the attention it deserves is the role the Union army played in helping to teach thousands of black soldiers and civilians in the South to read and write. The first important project for the education of blacks in the South was that headed by Edward L. Pierce of Boston. As Treasury Department superintendent of the cotton plantations in the South Carolina Sea Islands, Pierce in 1862 imported teachers (later called Gideonites) from the North to begin the work among the ten thousand black men, women, and children whom the islands' white population had left behind when they escaped before Union occupation in November 1861. General Sherman, the commander at Port Royal, wrote the War Department on 15 January 1862, urging "that suitable instructors be sent to the Negroes, to teach them all the rudiments of civilization."[25]

Because of their physical and cultural isolation, the blacks of the Sea Islands were among the most ignorant and backward of the entire South. Here indeed was a challenge to abolitionists, both black and white. Many northern men and women gave up comfortable homes and occupations to go south and teach the freedmen how to read and write. Elizabeth Botume, a white northern teacher to the Sea Islands, stated that she had difficulty in calling the roll because of the odd names, the lack of surnames, and the uncertainty of the children about their first names. These teachers encountered many trials and difficulties in their first months on the islands. The Sea Island blacks spoke a dialect that was very difficult for the northerners to understand. They also faced the task of trying to teach black children of all ages to read and write in overcrowded schoolrooms. After they learned to keep order and communicate with the pupils, teachers found to their delight that the children learned to read and write rapidly.

All of the freedmen showed great eagerness to learn to read and write. On the whole, most teachers were satisfied with the progress made by their students during the first year. Nearly twenty-five hundred children were taught in the day schools during the first few months, and almost the whole adult population attended Sunday schools.[26]

The most significant black teacher who came to the Sea Islands was Charlotte L. Forten of Philadelphia. Forten, a brilliant young black woman, had left her native city of Philadelphia in 1854 at age sixteen to attend the Higginson Grammar School in Salem, Massachusetts. She was determined to excell in all courses, not only to help herself but also to convince white Americans that blacks were capable of self-improvement if given the opportunity. Charles Lenox Remond, the proprietor of her foster home in Salem, was a prominent black abolitionist. His home served as headquarters for all anti-slavery lecturers passing through the city. Noted abolitionists such as William Lloyd Garrison, William Wells Brown, Wendell Phillips, and John Greenleaf Whittier visited Remond's home. Forten was constantly in contact with many abolitionists and she later attended abolitionist lecturers, fairs, and activities sponsored by the Salem Female Anti-Slavery Society.

Forten mastered her studies with an enthusiasm that won the respect of both teachers and pupils. She enrolled in the Salem Normal School after graduating with honors from the Higginson Grammar School. After completing her studies at the normal school, she was assigned a teaching position in the Epes Grammar School of Salem. She was the first black teacher to instruct white children in Salem. Forten's teaching position in Salem offered her an opportunity to pursue her real interests: abolitionism and learning. She began to lecture against slavery in many of the surrounding cities. She also won the friendship of Garrison, Phillips, Whittier, and other prominent abolitionists. Because of ill health, Forten later resigned her teaching position in Salem and returned to Philadelphia.[27]

With the outbreak of the Civil War, Forten saw a chance to serve her people as a teacher of freed slaves in the South. In August 1862, she requested to be sent to Port Royal as a teacher by the Philadelphia Port Royal Relief Association. In October 1862, Forten sailed from New York as an accredited agent for the association. There was some white prejudice against her in Port Royal shortly after she arrived. However, the prejudice against her soon disappeared after the whites discovered her talents and dedication. She was destined to prove that blacks were capable of self-improvement. Forten and her fellow teachers labored long hours to instruct these blacks in the three R's and other facets of their new status as freedmen. Forten returned to the North in May 1864 very proud of the progress the blacks on the Sea Islands had made. She kept a diary of her experiences in Port Royal. Her recollections are remarkable for the fact that she was one of few northern black teachers to have left a written account of her impressions.[28]

The Reverend James Lynch, a black Methodist minister from Baltimore, came to the South Carolina Sea Islands in 1863 and was appointed a government superintendent. He made a special appeal to northern blacks to serve as teachers on the Sea Islands. He stated that the white teachers were doing an excellent job of teaching the blacks on the Sea Islands, but he urged some blacks to come and help in this "holy mission." Many blacks responded to Lynch's appeal. The Reverend Henry M. Turner, pastor of Israel Bethel Church in Washington, D.C., declared in early 1863 that the time had arrived in the history of black Americans when grave responsibilities stared them in the face. The Emancipation Proclamation of President Lincoln had opened up a new series of obligations never known before. He also urged northern blacks to serve as teachers to the freedmen in the South, particularly on the Sea Islands. Many northern black churches sent teachers to the South Carolina Sea Islands.[29]

The Port Royal Experiment, as it came to be called, was regarded by abolitionists as a model that would demonstrate the capacity of slaves for freedom and the ability of reformers to educate and mold them into productive members of society. The Port Royal freedmen also industriously worked the land as they showed eagerness and ability to learn to read and write. However, as the war drew to a close and northern support subsided, many of the northern teachers returned to the North. Miss Laura Towne from Philadelphia and Miss Ellen Murray from Canada were two of the white teachers who remained. They had founded the Penn School, named after William Penn, on St. Helena Island in 1863. For nearly forty years after the war, Towne and Murray continued to teach the blacks on the island. Under their guidance, the Penn School graduates became leaders of the Sea Islands; many became teachers in the Penn School as well as in the other schools on the islands. With the exception

of the Penn School, the Port Royal freedmen were later betrayed
and the experiment was abondoned by most of its supporters when
President Johnson's postwar amnesty program dispossessed the
freedmen of most of their land.[30]

Susie King Taylor, previously mentioned, also served as a
teacher in the Union army. Taylor had been taught to read and
write secretly by Mrs. Mary Beasley, a free black friend of the
family. In April 1862, the Taylor family escaped to St. Simon's
Island for Union protection. One of the Union officers on the
island became aware of Taylor's talents and offered her the job
of taking charge of the school for the children on the island.
There were about six hundred men, women, and children on the
island. Taylor taught the children during the day and many of the
adults at night.

Taylor and the other contrabands on the island were later
transferred to the South Carolina Sea Islands. She was assigned
as a teacher in Colonel Thomas W. Higginson's Thirty-third
United States Colored Infantry. Taylor taught many of Higginson's
soldiers to read and write when they were off duty. The army
attracted many blacks because it gave them this opportunity to
learn to read and write. In fact, there was almost a religious
nature to the freedmen's regard for schooling.[31]

At first, the War Department made no formal declarations on
what was to be done with the starving and illiterate slaves as
they entered Union lines. However, Union officers, in an effort
to maintain order among their troops, tried various schemes to aid
the slaves. General Ulysses S. Grant made a systematic
response to the plight of blacks on 11 November 1862, when he
appointed John Eaton, Dartmouth graduate and a former school
superintendent, as Superintendent of Negro Affairs in the
Department of Tennessee (Tennessee, parts of Mississippi, and
Kentucky). Although concerned primarily with labor relations on
the plantations, Eaton attempted to attract instructors for the
former slaves. Adjutant General Lorenzo Thomas indicated the
War Department's support for the education of the freedmen on
29 September 1863, when he empowered Eaton to furnish teachers
with quarters, sustenance, and transportation. General Thomas
also authorized Eaton to confiscate the homes of rebels for use
as black schools. By 1865, more than 102 persons, including
many blacks, were teaching 6,267 pupils in 74 schools in the
Department of the Tennessee. It is significant that Eaton also

began to legalize marriage (marriage of blacks was not legal in slavery) among the freedmen to promote chastity and dignity in family relations.[32]

General Benjamin Butler instituted a similar program in his department for blacks. On 5 December 1863, he appointed Colonel J. B. Kinsman as Chief of a Department of Negro Affairs and directed him to furnish all possible aid to persons giving secular and religious instruction to the blacks in the Department of Virginia and North Carolina. Various benevolent associations provided school supplies and teachers while military authorities furnished schoolhouses, lodging, transportation, and food for the teachers. By July 1864, sixty-six teachers, including at least six blacks, were instructing three thousand black pupils in North Carolina alone.[33]

In December 1862, General Nathaniel P. Banks succeeded General Butler as commander of the Department of the Gulf (Louisiana, Mississippi, and Texas). General Banks, former Speaker of the United States House of Representatives and Governor of Massachusetts, instituted the most thorough of all systems for educating the freedmen in his department. In October 1863, Banks authorized a commission to take a census of blacks in his department and to establish schools for them in New Orleans. With the approval of the President, Banks issued on 22 March 1864 General Order No. 38 to govern the organization and growth of black schools in his department. The directive established a board of education for the Department of the Gulf, with Rush Plumly as general chairman and Lieutenant Edwin Wheelock as supervisor in Louisiana. Among other things, Banks empowered the board to establish schools in each parish; to select teachers and require them to attend an annual workshop conducted by the board; to regulate the curriculum; to levy a property tax to support the schools; and to provide books, at cost, to all black adults. By December 1864, the board of education was operating 95 schools with 9,571 children and 2,000 adults under the tutelage of 162 black and white teachers.[34]

Mrs. Mary D. Brice, a white teacher from Ohio, opened a free school for black children in New Orleans in 1862 after Union forces had occupied the city. A federal Commission of Enrollment, organized under Lieutenant William B. Stickney, encouraged other individuals to begin schools for the children of emancipated slaves, and by the beginning of 1864 eight such institutions had been established in New Orleans. One of them was under the direction of P. M. William, a black graduate of Dartmouth College.[35]

After the War Department began to recruit black soldiers in the South following the Emancipation Proclamation, many perplexing problems became apparent. First, it was difficult to recruit agents for communication with the illiterate former slaves. Second, the attempt to train them in warfare was very difficult Consequently, the officers of practically all the black regiments began to teach their troops in various ways. Colonel Higginson, commander of the Thirty-third United States Colored Infantry, appointed the chaplain as regimental teacher and Mrs. Mary Chamberlain as his assistant. In addition, the wives of many of the officers and men (including Susie King Taylor) were appointed teachers. Similarly, the men of the other black regiments attended schools conducted by their chaplains and northern black and white teachers. The desire for education was so strong among some of the black soldiers that many times they paid fifty cents to one dollar every month to hired teachers out of their seven dollars a month salary.[36]

Regiments of northern blacks were also participants in well-developed educational programs. Dr. Henry Bowditch, noted Boston black physician, organized a school for the men of the Fifty-fifth Massachusetts Infantry Regiment. Colonel James Beecher and his wife, Frances, established such an efficacious system of instruction in the Thirty-fifth that when the regiment was mustered out of service each man could proudly sign his name to the payroll. The blacks were so impressed by the instruction they received that the officers and men of the Sixty-second and Sixty-fifth contributed $6,380 to establish Lincoln University in Missouri. James Milton Turner, former slave and schoolteacher, was very instrumental in helping to establish Lincoln. After being wounded at the battle of Shiloh, Turner returned to Missouri where he had taught and, with the help of the two black regiments, raised funds to found Lincoln Institute. This small black college in Jefferson City welcomed all blacks, especially soldiers returning from the war.[37]

By the end of 1864, black soldiers had performed so well that the War Department on 3 December 1864 organized the all-black Twenty-fifth Army Corps from troops of the Department of Virginia and North Carolina under General Godfrey Weitzel. This became

84

the first and only all-black army corps in American military history. When General Butler united the thirty-seven regiments forming the Twenty-fifth Corps, he ordered the chaplains to conduct a school in each regiment. Thus, Butler guaranteed that 29,875 black soldiers would receive systematic instruction.[38]

The implementation of the blacks' overwhelming desire for education had several important consequences. Thousands of blacks received their first instruction in schools supervised or established by military authorities. In addition, teachers promoted the blacks' willingness to defend their civil and political rights by excellent performance on the battlefield. The educational ventures of the Union army were also important because they were the forerunners of the Freedmen's Bureau.[39]

In every northern city with a sizable black population the black churches and secular leaders formed freedmen's aid societies. A federal policy for relief of freedmen developed so slowly that private persons, both black and white, undertook to supplement it. As early as February 1862, meetings were held in many northern cities for the express purpose of rendering more effective aid to blacks in the South. On 22 February, the National Freedmen's Relief Association was organized in New York, and soon thereafter the Contraband Relief Association in Cincinnati. Within months many other aid societies were organized. Some of the larger and better known were the Contraband Relief Association of Washington, the Union Relief Association of the Israel Bethel Church in Washington, the Freedmen's Friend Society of Brooklyn, the African Civilization Society, in New York, and the Mother Bethel Church in Philadelphia. These associations solicited gifts of clothing and donations of cash. They distributed hundreds of barrels and boxes of donated clothing as well as food and medical supplies to needy contrabands.[40]

Elizabeth Keckley, Mrs. Lincoln's black seamstress, was the organizer of the Contraband Relief Association of Washington. Born a slave in Virginia, Mrs. Keckley had moved to St. Louis in the 1840s. She worked as a seamstress and dressmaker and purchased freedom for herself and her son in 1855. She later moved to Washington, where she came to the attention of Mrs. Lincoln and was given a job as the First Lady's modiste in 1861. Keckley soon became a close friend and confidante of Mrs. Lincoln.[41]

Keckley founded the Contraband Relief Association of Washington as a result of contact with destitute freedmen flocking into Washington during the summer of 1862. The idea of organizing a relief association came to her after witnessing a festival given for the benefit of the white sick and wounded soldiers of the city. On the following Sunday in church, she suggested that a society of black people be formed to work for the benefit of the destitute freedmen. The idea proved popular, and in two weeks the Contraband Relief Association was organized with forty working members. Keckley, as president of the association, traveled extensively securing money and donations of goods. Mrs. Lincoln and the President also made frequent contributions. Keckley developed a friendship with many prominent men, such as Frederick Douglass (who often lectured for the association), Wendell Phillips, and Reverend Henry H. Garnet. In its first two years the association spent more than sixteen hundred dollars and distributed over one hundred barrels and boxes of donated clothing to needy contrabands.[42]

During most of the war, Union administration of the contrabands was chaotic. Abolitionists began urging the government to adopt a uniform administrative policy toward the freedmen as soon as it became clear that the Civil War would result in some degree of emancipation. Not only were there different systems throughout the South of caring for the contrabands and utilizing their labor, but there were frequent conflicts of authority regarding freedmen's affairs between the Army and the Treasury Department.[43]

Under Secretary of War Simon Cameron and during Secretary Edwin Stanton's first months in office, no explicit policy for dealing with fugitives was given to field commanders. Each officer, lacking clear instructions, used his own discretion. Army officers throughout the South had assumed responsibility for the affairs of the blacks as a matter of military necessity. But Treasury Secretary Salmon P. Chase also claimed some authority over the freedmen because his department was in charge of abandoned lands and estates. For several months during the winter of 1861-62, Treasury Agent Edward L. Pierce had administered the affairs of the blacks at Port Royal. A dispute later erupted in the South Carolina Sea Islands between agents of the Treasury Department and military officers over the question of authority. There was a need for a unified policy in dealing with the large number of fugitives, abandoned land, and a labor system for the freedmen on abandoned and occupied land. Abolitionists recommended the creation of a federal bureau of emancipation to coordinate and administer to the needs of the freedmen, as well as provide protection and education for them.[44]

In early 1862, Secretary Stanton gave command of the Sea Islands project to General Rufus Saxton, with orders giving him extensive powers to take such measures, make such rules and regulations for the cultivation of the land, and for protection, employment, and government of the refugees as circumstances may require. Stanton, in his first weeks in office, had tried to interest a group of Congressmen in forming a commission to investigate the refugee problem. Nothing came of this proposal until the Radical leaders persuaded him to take it up again in early 1863. Accordingly, on 16 March the War Department created the American Freedmen's Inquiry Commission and authorized it to "investigate the condition of the colored population emancipated by acts of Congress and the President's proclamation of 1 January 1863, and to report what measures will best contribute to their protection and improvement, so that they may defend and support themselves."[45]

The Commission decided to visit personally as many freedmen's camps of the Union-occupied South as possible and send questionnaires to the areas they were unable to visit. The Commission later recommended the establishment of a freedmen's bureau to bring order out of the chaos of freedmen's affairs. The bureau should function at least until the end of the war, should supervise the employment and wage contracts of freedmen, and should establish courts to adjudicate disputes relating to freedmen. The Commission also emphasized the need for teaching the blacks self-reliance and establishing schools to be staffed by teachers from the freedmen's aid societies under the auspices of the proposed freedmen's bureau. Such guardianship by the bureau should be replaced as soon as possible by equal laws equally administered. The same civil and political rights enjoyed by whites should be granted to freedmen. If they were to become self-supporting, like the whites, they should have the same civil and political rights, stated the Commission.[46]

Senator Charles Sumner from Massachusetts was the real father of the American Freedmen's Inquiry Commission. Stanton had become a close friend and confidant of Sumner. Their liaison, particularly in matters concerning the blacks and conditions in the South, was a constant source of irritation to some of Stanton's colleagues in the administration. Sumner became the guiding force behind the new commission; Stanton merely established it. For more than a year the American Freedmen's Inquiry Commission functioned as an investigating body for the administration and as the eyes and ears of the Radicals in and out of Congress. Its official findings and recommendations set forth a comprehensive program for the dealing with the freedmen and with the South during and after the war. [47]

The Commission's recommendations laid the foundations for the Freedmen's Bureau. Frederick Douglass and other blacks became strong proponents of such a bureau. On 9 November 1863, officials of freedmen's aid societies of Philadelphia, Boston, and New York held a rally to bring pressure on the government in behalf of a freedmen's bureau. They also sent a delegation to meet with President Lincoln, as well as providing lobbyists for the bureau in Congress. After long debates in both houses of Congress, that centered mainly on the question of administration, the bill finally passed both houses, placing the bureau under the War Department, and was signed by Lincoln on 3 March 1865. The law established in the War Department a Bureau of Refugees, Freedmen, and Abandoned Lands to last for one year after the end of the war. The purposes were to dispense relief, supervise the labor of freed blacks, provide them with educational facilities, make rules and regulations for treatment, establish freedmen's courts, and settle the blacks on abandoned and confiscated lands. [48]

The commissioner of the bureau and as many as ten assistant commissioners were to be appointed by the President, with the consent of the Senate. Lincoln pondered for some time his selection of the head of the bureau. Abolitionists, both black and white, urged the President to give patient and conscientious attention to the selection of the head of the bureau. Salmon P. Chase, who had become Chief Justice of the Supreme Court, recommended General Rufus Saxton to the President. John Eaton and James E. Yeatman were also recommended. Lincoln offered the post to James Yeatman, who was well known in black-relief circles. His experience with the Western Sanitary Commission had made him thoroughly familiar with the sources of charity and the kind of organizations the bureau would have to depend upon. His efforts to improve conditions in the contraband camps also marked him as a man who would try to run the bureau for the sake of the blacks. However, Yeatman declined the President's offer.

Lincoln's final choice of a commissioner was based on the recommendation of Secretary of War Stanton, who recommended Oliver Otis Howard. However, the appointment was delayed until Howard could leave his command in the field. Until 26 April 1865, he was commanding general of the Army of the Tennessee. Although Lincoln was dead before Howard gave up his command, his successor, Andrew Johnson, appointed Howard Commissioner of the Freedmen's Bureau because Stanton told him Lincoln had decided to offer the post to Howard.[49]

The Freedmen's Bureau was an attempt to establish a government guardianship over the blacks of the South and insure their economic and civil rights. Its establishment was a herculean task both physically and socially, and it not only met the solid opposition of the white South, but even the North looked at it as socialistic and overpaternal.[50] Nevertheless, the bureau aided refugees and freedmen by furnishing supplies and medical services, supervising contracts between freedmen and their employers, and managing confiscated and abondoned lands. The bureau also resettled many people who had been displaced by the war. There can be no doubt that the Freedmen's Bureau relieved much suffering among blacks and whites. Between 1865 and 1869, for example, the bureau issued twenty-one million rations, approximately five million going to whites and fifteen million to blacks. The bureau achieved its greatest success, however, in education. It set up or supervised all kinds of schools: day, night, Sunday, and industrial schools, as well as colleges. It cooperated closely with philanthropic and religious organizations in the North in the establishment of many institutions. Among the schools founded in this period which received aid from the bureau were Howard University, Fisk University, Hampton Institute, St. Augustine's College, Atlanta University, Storer College, and Johnson C. Smith University.[51]

The Civil War accelerated black Americans' drive for civil rights and desegregation in the North. Discrimination against blacks and the firmly held belief in the superiority of the white race were not restricted to the South but were shared by an overwhelming majority of white Americans in the North. Abraham Lincoln, in his vigorous support of both white supremacy and denial of equal rights for blacks, simply gave expression to almost universal American convictions. It was generally believed that the superior white race, with its roots deep in the experiences of law and government, had the obligation of teaching the inferior black race, with its history of four thousand years of barbarism, the precious knowledge of citizenship. Therefore, despite the absence of slavery in the North, freedom did not confer citizenship. [52]

In most parts of the North in 1860, black men did not enjoy equal rights. Blacks could vote on equal terms with whites in only five states: Maine, New Hampshire, Vermont, Massachusetts, and Rhode Island. These states contained only seven percent of the northern population. In New York State, blacks could vote only if they owned two hundred fifty dollars worth of property. About twenty-one percent of the state's adult male blacks qualified under this provision. No such restriction was placed on white suffrage. Several states prohibited blacks from testifying against whites in court. This law gave free license to whites to rob, beat, and kill blacks without fear of arrest. Public accommodations, transportation facilities, restaurants, hotels, and theaters in some parts of the North were segregated. Blacks were barred from jury service in every state except Massachusetts. Public schools in most of the northern cities were segregated. Although some white schools admitted blacks, most northern states either excluded them altogether or established separate schools for them. Blacks also suffered discrimination in housing and jobs in every part of the North. [53]

The most eloquent and persistent spokesmen for the revolution of racial equality during the war were Frederick Douglass and Wendell Phillips. Douglass was a black abolitionist orator, journalist, and spokesman for his people. He lectured all over the North in behalf of emancipation and equal rights. Douglass reached the minds and hearts of white people more effectively than any other man of his race. His monthly journal was read by many anti-slavery whites, and his lectures drew large numbers of white people. Douglass saw the coming of the war as a crusade for freeing the slaves; therefore, he urged black men to form militia companies and advised Lincoln to enlist blacks. Too old to bear arms himself, Douglass served as a recruiting agent, traveling throughout the North exhorting blacks to sign up. He was especially proud of enrolling two of his sons. [54]

Douglass had several meetings with President Lincoln during the war to discuss slavery, enlistment of blacks in the Union army, discrimination against black soldiers, civil rights for blacks, and other issues related to blacks. As the war drew to a close, Douglass concentrated his efforts on suffrage for the freedmen. It was his belief that the newly freed blacks must have the vote in order to protect and maintain their liberty. He lived to see most of the demands he had made before, during, and immediately after the Civil War become the law of the land. Unfortunately, he also lived to see many of these laws, particularly the Fourteenth and Fifteenth Amendments, become dead-letters.[55]

Wendell Phillips was an American orator and reformer. He was a graduate of Harvard Law School, and was admitted to the bar in 1834, but he took little interest in the legal profession. He became a confirmed abolitionist and follower of William Lloyd Garrison. He had come to prominence with a fiery speech in Boston on 8 December 1837, at a meeting called to protest the murder of the abolitionist Elizah P. Lovejoy at Alton, Illinois. From that time to the Civil War he served in most matters as Garrison's lieutenant and was perhaps the most effective orator in the movement. He was one of the finest speakers of his century and was much in demand as a lecturer. He lectured for antislavery societies and wrote editorials and pamphlets.[56]

Phillips assailed Lincoln's reluctancy to uproot the institution of slavery, and after emancipation he contended that blacks should be guaranteed full civil rights. As early as December 1861, Phillips stated that he envisioned a United States in which there were no whites, no blacks, no southerners, no northerners, only American citizens with one impartial law over all.[57]

Blacks throughout the North organized associations which sponsored lecturers, provided legal assistance to blacks, and served as a pressure group in behalf of the interests of all black people. The emergence of a national policy of arming blacks to fight for the Union gave an important boost to the antisegregation efforts. The antislavery press began to publish stories of discrimination and segregation against blacks.[58]

The Civil War produced great changes in the status of northern blacks. Some of the more important gains for civil rights during the war were made on the national level. Under the leadership of Charles Sumner, Congress passed several anti-discrimination measures during the war. In 1862 the Senate repealed an 1825 law barring blacks from carrying mail, which later passed the House and became law. Congress also decreed that in all proceedings of the District of Columbia courts there must be no exclusion of witnesses because of race, and in 1864 this legislation was broadened to cover every federal court in the nation.

At the state level, black leaders were active in the movement to end discrimination and segregation. California blacks worked hard to obtain a repeal of the law barring blacks from testifying against whites. Their efforts were rewarded in 1863 when the California legislature repealed the law. Blacks could henceforth testify in any court case in California. Blacks could not testify against whites in Illinois, but the most severe feature of the Illinois "black laws," as they were commonly called, was the law barring black immigration. Every black person entering the state with intent to settle was subject to a heavy fine; in default of payment he could be sold at public auction to the person bidding the shortest period of service in return for payment of the fine. Blacks in Chicago, under the leadership of John Jones, formed the Repeal Association in 1864. This association circulated a petition and obtained eleven thousand signatures which Jones later carried to Springfield to the state legislature. Jones made a very impressive speech to the legislature concerning discriminatory laws in Illinois. The contribution of black soldiers to Union victory had produced a favorable climate for Jones's appeal, and the legislature in February 1865 repealed the laws barring black immigration and testimony.[59]

Legal barriers fell rapidly in most parts of the North during or immediately after the Civil War, but other forms of discrimination proved more resistent. Blacks in Philadelphia under the leadership of William Still, mounted an attack against streetcar segregation. The City of Brotherly Love was one of the most rigidly segregated cities of the North. Most of Philadelphia's streetcars allowed blacks to ride only on the front platform; some refused to admit blacks at all. Blacks and white abolitionist organizations repeatedly petitioned the Board of Railway Presidents and the state legislature to end streetcar segregation, but to little avail. Black contribution to Union victory on the battlefield made the cruelty and injustice of the Jim Crow policy more and more obvious, and by the winter of 1864-65 the Republican party and the Republican press in Philadelphia were supporting the drive to end streetcar segregation. In 1867 streetcar segregation ended in Philadelphia. It had ended in

Washington, D.C., two years before. Blacks deserve much of the credit for these triumphs, because they initiated the drive and kept up the pressure until streetcar segregation ended throughout the northern cities.[60]

Blacks also attempted to improve and desegregate education in the North during the war. Many northern cities maintained segregated public schools in 1861. Blacks were dissatified with segregated, inferior education for their children and began to launch a drive to break down racial barriers in public schools. The quest for equal educational opportunities by blacks prompted some strong and frequently violent protests in the North. The possibility that black children would be mixed with white children in the same classroom provoked widespread fears and prejudices. The admission of blacks to white schools, opponents maintained, would result in violence and prove fatal to public education. Moreover, many alleged that black children, degraded, semibarbaric, and immoral, would have an injurious effect on their children and would teach them vicious habits. However, blacks continued to send petitions to school boards, city councils, and state legislatures. They also pressured politicians and kept the issue before the public. As a result of their efforts, many northern state legislatures and local public school boards outlawed school segregation during or immediately after the war. Many forms of legal and social discrimination were also broken down by blacks in the North. Massachusetts enacted the first comprehensive public accommodations law in America in 1865, forbidding the exclusion of any person because of race or color from restaurants, inns, theaters, and places of amusement. Several other states adopted similar legislation shortly after the Civil War.[61]

The desire for desegration was also voiced by intelligent southern blacks. New Orleans blacks fought against segregation throughout the war years. The longest and one of the most bitter of the blacks' campaigns for equal treatment in New Orleans involved public transportation. The first issue which arose involved the "star cars" which were exclusively for blacks on the streetcar lines in New Orleans. In their campaign to abolish the star cars, blacks insisted that their exclusion from the "white cars" was not only humiliating and an inconvenience (many times whites crowded the black cars leaving little room for black passengers) but stamped the mark of inferiority on them. Blacks began to petition military officials for a redress of this

93

segregation as early as 1862. The leading black newspapers began to urge blacks to enter the cars set aside for whites, and almost frequently as they boarded the "white cars" they were beaten and thrown off. Whites in New Orleans maintained that blacks and whites were so dissimilar that it was impossible for them to interact on terms of equality. Blacks were afflicted with so many vices and were so inferior to whites that they should be kept in a subordinate position socially, politically, and economically.[62]

As early as 1862 many abolitionists, including blacks, had also come to the conclusion that there could be no security for the freedmen without black suffrage. However, suffrage for the newly emancipated slaves seemed to be an impractical idea to many in 1862-63. Yet Wendell Phillips and Frederick Douglass had already begun the movement to require black suffrage as a condition of reconstruction. Abolitionists vehemently opposed Lincoln's long-awaited policy of restoration which he announced on 8 December 1863. Under his constitutional authority to grant pardons for offenses against the United States, Lincoln offered full pardon and restoration of property, except slaves, to those engaged in rebellion who would swear an oath of allegiance to the United States and to all laws and proclamations concerning slavery. Civil and diplomatic officials of the Confederate government, high army and navy officers, and certain other prominent Confederates were exempted from this offer. Whenever in any state the number of voters taking the oath reached ten percent of the number who had voted in the 1860 elections, this loyal nucleus could reestablish a state government to which Lincoln promised executive recognition. The President further stated that "any provision which may be adopted by such State government in relation to the freed people of such State, which shall recognize and declare their permanent freedom, provide for their education, and which may yet be consistent, as a temporary arrangement, with their present condition as a laboring, landless, and homeless class, will not be objected to by the national Executive." Many abolitionists interpreted this to mean that southern whites would be allowed to handle the race problem in their own way; simply by adopting a temporary apprenticeship system they could exclude blacks from equal civil and political rights.[63]

Phillips and Douglass were the most persistent critics of the administration's reconstruction program. They argued that this nation would never be what it should be until every citizen possessed the ballot. Douglass maintained that the administration had to take an uncompromising stand on the following points concerning the aims of the war: that slavery be abolished; that everyone in the country be entitled to the same rights, protection, and opportunities; and that black men should be invested with the right to vote and to hold office. Lincoln and most Republicans, however, opposed admitting blacks to the ranks of voters, jurors, or officeholders. During 1864 more and more abolitionists began to condemn Lincoln's reconstruction policy. Under pressure, Lincoln later suggested that some of the blacks, the very intelligent and those who had fought gallantly in the war, might be allowed suffrage. Most abolitionists, however, wanted qualifications which were applied equally to both races. One rule must be applied to all, or no rule must be made, stated the abolitionists.[64]

Education and the ballot for the freedmen were two of the most important abolitionist requirements for a sound reconstruction of the South. However, many abolitionists realized that political equality and education would mean little to the freedmen without a solid foundation of economic independence. Many advocated land for the freedmen or otherwise the white planters would keep the blacks in a state of semi-serfdom by paying them low wages and making them economically dependent on the whites. Many abolitionists also stated that Confederate landowners had forfeited their property as well as their other rights and privileges by taking up arms against the Union. They urged the administration to confiscate Confederate land and allot a portion of it to the landless. The Confiscation Act of July 1862, as originally passed by Congress, met many of the abolitionists' demands. It provided for the permanent confiscation of all property belonging to traitors; however, this act was later weakened by a joint resolution of Congress which declared that the property would revert to the heirs after the life of the offenders.[65]

When emancipation became an official northern war aim in 1863, abolitionist demands for land for the landless in the South became more insistent. Senator Charles Sumner introduced a bill in February 1863, to grant ten acres of land to every black soldier in the South. The bill did not pass, but it was a sign of the increasing congressional concern over the land question in the South. Many Americans believed that the freedmen had earned a grant of land by long years of suffering and toil. In March 1863, some 16,749 acres of abandoned plantation lands on the Sea Islands were put up for general sale. About 2,000 acres were purchased by freedmen who had saved their wages and pooled their savings. The remainder of the land was bought by northern investors and speculators. The sale of nearly ninety percent of this land to outsiders created considerable dissatisfaction among the freedmen. Some blacks who had saved a little money, but were unable to pay competitive prices for the land on which they had worked most of their lives, were sadly disappointed. At second public auction of nearly 60,000 acres of land in February 1864, the freedmen were able to buy only about 2,750 acres.[66]

General William T. Sherman created a revolutionary land reform program in his "Order No. 15." As he marched through Georgia in the last month of 1864, thousands of ragged and destitute freedmen straggled along behind his troops. When the army reached Savannah the problem of taking care of these refugees became very critical. The refugees were victims of malnutrition, diseases, and exposure. Secretary of War Stanton, who was visiting Savannah, held a conference with Sherman and other officials to discuss the problems of the freedmen. Stanton made known his desire to speak directly with representative of the freedmen. On 12 January 1865, he met with twenty black leaders at Sherman's headquarters and asked their opinion on the problems involving their welfare. Among these black leaders were ministers, pilots, sailors, and former overseers of cotton and rice plantations.[67]

The black leaders offered Stanton sound and wise advice based on a knowledgeable understanding of the problems. When Stanton asked, quite significantly, whether they preferred living scattered in communities of mixed white and black settlements or in an area restricted to blacks entirely, with the exception of one, the blacks agreed that they preferred to live by themselves. They stated that prejudice against them in the South was so strong that it would take years to overcome. This conference and Stanton's other investigations resulted in the issuance of Sherman's famous Special Field Orders No. 15 on 16 January 1865 with the full concurrence of the Secretary of War. The whole Sea Island region, from Charleston southward to Jacksonville, and the coastal lands thirty miles inland were designated for exclusive black settlement. Freedmen settling in this area could take tracts of land not exceeding forty acres per family. The blacks would receive possessory titles to these lands until Congress later regulated the titles. No white persons, except authorized military personnel, would be allowed in the area.[68]

General Rufus Saxton was appointed by Sherman to supervise the settlement of blacks on the land and to have full power over the freedmen's affairs in this area. After full assurance by Sherman that the arrangement would be permanent and would not result in another breach of faith, Saxton accepted the appointment and began settling blacks on the land. Blacks also wanted to know the nature of the titles the government would give them and what assurance they would have that the land would be theirs after they improved it. Considering the condition of the neglected fields and the ruined economy of the islands, these questions were very important to them. After assurance from Saxton that land titles would be forthcoming, the blacks organized themselves with rudimentary tools and seeds, and began clearing land for spring planting. They also began building homes and laying out plans for villages.[69]

Abolitionist reaction to this experiment varied. Some commended General Sherman and Secretary Stanton for granting land to the freedmen, but disliked the feature of setting the blacks apart from the whites. Many argued that this resembled colonization and asserted that, if the blacks were good enough to live in the presence of white men as slaves, they should be good enough to dwell in their presence as freemen. Secretary Stanton sent a private letter to William L. Garrison, a leading abolitionist, pointing out that the black leaders themselves had expressed a desire to be set apart from whites. Stanton also enclosed the minutes of the meeting with the Savannah blacks, which Garrison later published in the _Liberator_ along with a defense of (Sherman' order.[70]

Some abolitionists were afraid that white teachers and missionaries would not be allowed in the black settlement. General Saxton pointed out that the segregation aspect of the order had been designed to keep out speculators, slick traders, and other whites who might take advantage of the freedmen. He further stated that they would admit white teachers, officials of freedmen's aid societies, and other whites who had legitimate business in the area.[71]

These assurances were welcomed by suspicious abolitionists and converted them to strong supporters of the experiment. Thousands of Georgia, South Carolina, and Florida freedmen were settled on the land. By the end of the war over thirty thousand blacks had been settled on the coastal lands. Many of them had planted good crops on their new land. The experiment seemed to be a success. But this experiment was destroyed by President Andrew Johnson, who in August 1865 issued orders of pardon and restoration of property to the former Confederate owners of these lands. Most of the blacks were turned off their farms and a majority of them were compelled to work for the white landowners. (Frederick Douglass later cited the refusal of the government to provide the freedmen with an opportunity to obtain good land of their own as the main reason for their helplessness in years to come.[72])

The ownership of land was very important to the freedmen. To the predominantly rural southern black the ownership of land was the chief mark of a free man. To permit blacks to buy land, however, was not the common practice. Throughout the South the prevailing pattern was for the Federal government to take title to the land and then lease it to whites, either resident planters who took the oath of allegiance or northerners who came South. However, a few blacks were able to lease land.[73]

The best known plantation under black lessees was Davis Bend. This fertile strip of land was formerly the property of Joseph Davis, the oldest brother of Jefferson Davis. Before the war Joseph Davis was impressed with the ideas of Robert Owen, the British industrialist and social reformer, concerning utopian communities. Davis, a prominent lawyer in Natchez, Mississippi, read extensively to keep abreast of the reform sentiment then prevalent among intellectuals in England and New England. He later began to probe Owen's thoughts for a blueprint which might prove applicable to his own situation. Davis purchased a peninsula of eleven thousand acres of rich bottom land on the Mississippi some thirty miles from Vicksburg, which came to be called Davis Bend. At the age of forty-two, he married a sixteen-year-old girl from New Orleans. He later gave up his highly successful law practice and retired to Davis Bend where he proposed to establish a model prosperous plantation community. This model community was based on his conviction that all men, white and black, were capable of living harmonious productive lives through rational cooperation.[74]

By the 1850s Joseph Davis had created at Davis Bend the kind of cotton plantation that was the goal of most ambitious young men of the Deep South.[75] He owned three hundred forty-five slaves which put Davis in the top twelve percent of Mississippi slaveowners. Davis treated his slaves very humanely. Their quarters were well constructed and much larger than other slave quarters in the South. Unlike fellow slaveowners, Davis sought to maintain order and productivity by gaining the cooperation of his slave community through a form of self-government. He established a court where a slave jury heard complaints of slave misconduct and the testimony of the accused in his own defense. No slave was punished except upon conviction by this jury of his peers; Davis sat as the judge. Not only did the court adjudicate disputes among the slaves but it also reviewed complaints from the overseers, who could not punish anyone without court permission. Davis also permitted his slaves to sell produce such as chickens, eggs, vegetables, and wood from the swamps on the market from their labor beyond the field work. He provided special rewards for superior performance in the fields. Special feasts were always provided for holidays.

According to Janet Hermann, the experiment by Joseph Davis was a great success. In the fertile Mississippi bottom lands, Davis developed a plantation that was among the most prosperous in the state. Although cotton was the major cash crop, Davis raised a wide variety of crops. There were no slave runaways which indicated that the slaves were fairly satisfied. Nor is there any evidence of open discontent among the slaves. To the contrary, evidence indicates an unusual affection for the master and his family. In spite of all the special treatment enjoyed by blacks at Davis Bend, they were still aware that they were not free.[76]

The Civil War destroyed Davis's model plantation experiment and replaced it first with chaos and then with several innovative communities established by Union officers. By the spring of 1864, seventy-five free black families, representing a total population of some six hundred, had settled on the plantation. Each family worked plots of from five to one hundred acres. Rations and teams were furnished by the government, to be paid for when the crop was marketed. Davis Bend was practically self-governing, the military officers in charge permitted the blacks to handle their own court procedure and prescribe penalties for wrongdoing. The Davis Bend freedmen raised a variety of crops, including corn, vegetables, melons, and cotton. They also sold hogs, chickens, eggs, and fish to the soldiers and the commissary. Davis Bend settlers became fairly prosperous. Near the end of the war Davis Bend became a haven for fleeing freedmen as well as a contraband camp. They were crowded into inadequate accommodations there and a great deal of sickness and diseases occurred.[77]

The blacks as freemen in the South underwent many changes during the war. They were legally married for the first time. Under slavery, parents were unable to discharge the full responsibilities of parenthood since slave marriages were not legal and slave families faced daily the threat of separation. Marriage was regarded as a privilege and an obligation that came with freedom, and the former slaves showed their readiness for this obligation. Families who had been forcibly separated sought their former mates, going from one plantation to another. More than three thousand couples married in Vicksburg during an eight-month period in 1864. Black marriages were performed by chaplains and northern missionaries in the freedmen's camps almost from the beginning of the war. Yet, it was not until 1865 that the states began to accept black marriages as legal. Under slavery some men had been bigamously "married" to more than one wife, having remarried every time they were sold to another plantation. When freedom came the question arose as to which woman the man should legally marry. In the Sea Islands, General Saxton advised that the man marry the "wife" who had borne the most children.[78]

The marriages of the freedmen caused them to take family names. Under slavery the blacks had first names only; in several southern states slaves were flogged for assuming a family name. Black marriages and the assumption of family names also made it possible for them to legally record births and deaths. The wholesale system of surnames for freedmen started during the Spring of 1862 by General Ormsby M. Mitchel. He advised the blacks under his command to take the last names of their former masters. Many freedmen, as well as former owners, were not happy with this method of selecting surnames. According to Bobby Lovett, many blacks in Tennessee took the names of important people and places. Some of the names were those used by the slaves during slavery, but kept secret from the master: Prince, Duke, King, Love, Strong, and Black. Lovett further states that the Civil War freed the black Tennessee family, legalized it, and recorded its roots in the county record books.[79]

Religion had been an important part of black life in the South before the Civil War and it remained an important part during the war. Free blacks in the cities of the South had a few churches. For many of them the church was the most important institution in the community. With emancipation of the blacks began to enjoy more religious liberty and the right to control their own churches. Almost immediately after Union troops occupied the cities of the South, blacks began to form new churches. The blacks in the contraband camps held regular religious services under the auspices of a missionary minister, army chaplain, or black preacher. Most contraband camp school buildings also served as the housing for the church. Black soldiers held religious services, too, and their chaplains were quite influential with the black soldiers.[80]

Prior to the Civil War, slaves had commonly attended white churches where their masters worshipped. Because the war broke up the relationship of master and slave, it induced the freedmen to leave the master's church and form their own. Northern missionaries, black and white, were especially significant in helping the former slaves organize churches and train their ministers. One of the most important and distinctive features of the black church was the singing of spiritual songs. These songs had been created by the slaves and were filled with pathos, joy, pain, and suffering. The whole religious service reflected their belief in the presence and power of God. Their services, a mixture of grief and sadness about their weary life on earth, provided an emotional release for them. The sermons and songs about their bondage, and the passionate prayers for Divine aid, gave to their services a reality, vividness, and emotionalism which created a sense of shared suffering and hope which caused the congregation to shout, cry, and raise a joyful noise to the Lord.[81]

Even though most blacks could not vote in presidential elections, many did not endorse Lincoln for a second term. Some blacks, including Frederick Douglass, were critical of the President because of his seemingly conservative approach to the question of reconstruction and black suffrage. They also pointed to Lincoln's reluctance to take decisive action against slavery in 1861-62, his suppression of emancipation edicts issued by some of his generals, his efforts to colonize the blacks, and the injustices to black troops. They further stated that Lincoln's reconstruction policy would soon restore the former Confederates to power and leave the freedmen little better off than under slavery.

Douglass gave his support to a call by radical Republicans and abolitionists for a convention to oppose the renomination of Lincoln. The convention met on 31 May 1864 in Cleveland and nominated John C. Fremont for president and John Cochrane for vice-president. The Republicans met on 8 June, under the name of the National Union Party, in Baltimore. They nominated Lincoln and Andrew Johnson, the War Democrat from Tennessee, for vice-president. The divided Republican party opened up the possibility of a Democratic victory. However, two events at the end of August and the beginning of September radically changed the political situation and caused most Republicans and blacks to unite behind the President. On 30 August the Democrats nominated George B. McClellan for president on an anti-emancipation peace platform, and on 3 September Atlanta fell to General Sherman. McClellan now symbolized despair, defeatism, and the continuance of slavery. The prestige of the Lincoln administration sky-rocketed. Fremont withdrew from the race and Frederick Douglass came out publicly in support of the President.[82]

Nearly every northern black who could vote in November cast his ballot for Lincoln. After Lincoln's re-election some blacks continued to worry about the President's conservatism on the reconstruction issue. However, by the spring of 1865, Lincoln had begun to move toward accepting some of the demands of the blacks on reconstruction. The President's assassination on 14 April 1865 came as a shattering blow to blacks. Frederick Douglass was among those who eulogized him. Most black Americans had come to look upon Lincoln as a great president and a friend to black people. Despite the disappointment of Lincoln's lenient amnesty program, the assassination of the President silenced his black critics and threw a stunned black community into deep mourning. The President's initial doubts about emancipation and the enlistment of blacks in the Union army were now forgotten, his equivocation on civil rights ignored, and his schemes on colonization forgiven. To most blacks, they had lost a friend and protector.[83]

Except for the sorrow produced by Lincoln's assassination, the mood of the blacks at the end of the war was optimistic. For the war, with all its bloodshed and sorrow, was an emancipating and uplifting national experience. Its most striking achievement was not the battle conquests on sea and land, but the momentum it gave to the ideals of the freedom and the dignity of man.

CHAPTER V

SUMMARY AND CONCLUSION

The Revolution of 1775-1783 created the American nation and the Civil War of 1861-1865 preserved this nation from destruction and determined, in large measure, what kind of nation it would be. Black Americans played a major role in the total Union war effort in preserving the nation. Unfortunately, the contributions made by black Americans toward helping the Union win the Civil War have been almost totally excluded from the texts used in the public schools.

Shortly after the fall of Fort Sumter, black Americans answered President Lincoln's call for volunteers to suppress the rebellion but were turned away. Despite the fact that black soldiers had fought with distinction in the Revolution and the War of 1812, state constitutions barred blacks from serving in most state militias and no blacks were in the regular army at this time. Blacks throughout the North insisted that they should be permitted to enlist in the Union army. Many black leaders took the initiative in recruiting black soldiers in anticipation of later active service in the Union army, but they were told that "this is a white man's war" and ordered by police officials to discontinue recruitment and drilling exercises. Public opinion in 1861, except perhaps in a few of the New England states, was overwhelmingly opposed to allowing blacks in the militia or the army as soldiers. From the beginning, President Lincoln made clear that his central purpose was to preserve the Union. He assured North and South that he would not interfere with slavery. While abolitionists, both black and white, called for an end to slavery and the use of black soldiers, Lincoln was concerned with keeping the loyalty of the four border states that remained in the Union. He also believed that most northerners would not support a war to end slavery.

The northern black man's eagerness to serve in the Union army, even though he was denied becoming a soldier, was vividly illustrated by his services in other capacities. Some joined the navy, as the navy had never kept free blacks from enlisting. Others, determined to serve in the army, went as waiters, cooks, teamsters, and laborers. To many blacks in the South, the war went hand-in-hand with freedom. Deserting slaves began to enter Union lines seeking freedom shortly after the war started. The

United States government had no clear policy regarding the
deserting slaves. Slaves as property were recognized and
sustained by the Constitution. However, the Union policy
toward the slaves began to change. General Benjamin Butler on
23 May 1861 declared three fugitive slaves that had constructed
Confederate defenses in Hampton, Virginia, as contraband of war.
The news of Butler's contraband decision quickly became known
to the slaves of the South and they began to enter the Union lines
in large numbers. The fugitives entering Union lines inevitably
increased as the Union armies pushed farther into Confederate
heartland. Soon these fugitives were performing most of the
various services needed around the army camps. They were used
as teamsters, cooks, officers' servants, and laborers.

Abolitionists, both black and white, urged the President to
free and employ the blacks as soldiers. Some members of
Congress also began to pressure the President. In July and
August, 1861, Congress passed measures which declared that all
slaves whose masters had permitted them to be used in the
military or naval service of the Confederacy forfeited. Some of
the Union commanders in the slave states began to free the
slaves in their departments.

By early 1862, it had become clear that a permanent program
for the care and employment of arriving blacks into Union lines
had to be established. Blacks were coming into Union lines by
the thousands. Special camps (contraband camps) were set up to
aid these blacks. Though conditions in many of these camps
were deplorable, they provided sources of labor for the Union
army.

Edwin Stanton, who replaced Simon Cameron as Secretary of
War in January 1862, believed that the Confederacy was a
conspiracy of traitors and that total war was necessary to destroy
it. Aid, emancipation, and the military use of blacks became
weapons of war for him. Stanton could not sympathize with
Lincoln's cautious approach to these problems. Thus, he turned
to the radical leaders in Congress for support in an attempt to
wage total war against the South and in dealing with the refugees.

Lincoln believed slavery was wrong; however, he held that
the Presidency did not confer on him the right to act upon his own
feelings and beliefs. He attempted several solutions to the
slavery problem including payments to slave masters from the

national treasury for freeing their slaves, federal compensation to states that had adopted a plan of gradual abolition of slavery, and colonization of the blacks outside the country.

By mid-1862 there was a strong feeling manifested all over the North in favor of freeing the slaves, and in many quarters the arming of blacks were regarded with favor. In the summer of 1862 Union forces suffered a series of military defeats. Mounting casualties, the returning wounded veterans, the alarming increase in desertions, and the growing difficulty in obtaining enlistments led to a reassessment of the military value of emancipation and black recruitment. The slaves of the enemy also represented a source of strength. Despite the government's official opposition on black soldiers, several Union generals began to organize black regiments.

There was still considerable opposition in the North to the enlistment of black soldiers, but on 25 August 1862 the War Department, nevertheless, authorized General Rufus Saxton, military governor of the South Carolina Sea Islands, to raise five regiments of black troops on the islands. The First South Carolina Volunteers regiment was soon formed and Thomas W. Higginson was appointed its commander. This was the first official black regiment mustered into the Union army. This act signified a major turning point in the war policy of the Lincoln administration.

In the early days of September 1862 a sense of despondency settled heavily upon the northern people. General Pope's loss of the second Battle of Bull Run was a fearful blow. But on 17 September General George B. McClellan turned back General Robert E. Lee's invasion of Maryland at Sharpsburg. Seizing upon this as the victory for which he had waited, the President unexpectedly issued his preliminary Emancipation Proclamation five days later.

Not until his final proclamation on 1 January 1863 did Lincoln publicly endorse the use of blacks as soldiers. The administration became thoroughly committed to the use of black troops during the next several months after the Emancipation Proclamation. By December 1863 over fifty thousand blacks had enrolled in the Union army and this number increased rapidly as Union troops moved deeper into the Confederacy.

A great expansion of black recruiting activity took place in 1864, but already in 1863 the policy of black enlistment had proven itself a success. Black soldiers in 1863 fought courageously at Port Hudson, Milliken's Bend, Fort Wagner, and Moscow Station. By the end of the Civil War more than 186,000 black men had served in the Union army.[1] They participated in 449 battles and served in nearly every military department of the United States army. Approximately 37,330 black soldiers lost their lives while serving in the Union army and 17 blacks were awarded Congressional Medals of Honor for outstanding bravery. Testimony to the martial valor of the black soldiers came from friends as well as enemies. They exhibited the highest qualities of soldiership in major engagements too numerous to mention.

While the black soldiers were fighting creditably for Union survival on the battlefield, black sailors were also performing their duties effectively during battle action. Blacks constituted twenty-five percent (29,511) of the total naval personnel. Four black sailors were awarded the Congressional Medal of Honor for outstanding bravery in combat conditions. Their contribution, particularly in terms of information concerning the enemy's potential, disposition, and terrain, was invaluable.

Of the thousands of slaves who escaped and came into the Union navy the most spectacular was Robert Smalls and his party. They seized the Planter, a three hundred ton Confederate steamer heavily loaded with munitions of war, food, and other supplies, and delivered it to the Union. William Tillman, another black man, performed another spectacular naval exploit by saving the Union schooner S. J. Waring from Confederate capture. The Waring was a vessel of three hundred tons of assorted cargo bound in early July 1861 for South America. Mary Louvestre was also one of the unsung black heroines of the Union navy. Mary, a trusted slave, overheard conversations between her master, who was an engineer, and other high ranking Confederate engineers concerning the remodeling of the Merrimac. They stated that this vessel, which would be completed in a few months, would be able to destroy the Union navy. Mary managed to get a copy of the secret designs from her master's office and took it to Washington. The Union navy was not destroyed as a result of Mary Louvestre's spectacular naval exploit.

While more than two hundred thousand black Americans in uniforms were performing their duties creditable on the battlefield and seacoast, black civilians were not neglectful of home-front responsibilities. They also performed their duties creditably and made valuable contributions to the Union war efforts.

The Union spy system relied heavily upon information supplied by former slaves. Allan Pinkerton, founder and chief of the National Secret Service, stated that he found the blacks of invaluable assistance from the very beginning of the war. John Scobell, a former Mississippi slave, became one of Pinkerton's most trusted agents for the Army of the Potomac. As a spy, Scobell made many daring missions into the South securing valuable information which Pinkerton submitted to the military high command. George Scott, Henry Blake, Mary Elizabeth Bowser, Harriet Tubman, and William Jackson were also prominent black spies for the Union. Union generals frequently obtained valuable information on the location and size of enemy forces from contrabands who entered their lines. The blacks of the South were acquainted with the roads, paths, fords, and other natural features of the country; thus, they made excellent spies, scouts, and guides.

Another very important contribution of blacks to the Union cause was their labor. During the war there were more than two hundred thousand black civilians in the service of the Union armies as laborers. Blacks performed a variety of duties as laborers. They constructed roads, railroads, and bridges. Thousands were employed as blacksmiths, woodchoppers, servants, cooks, gravediggers, teamsters, loaders and unloaders of supplies, as well as performing many other duties. Blacks were also excellent foragers. The Union armies, fighting and marching in enemy territory, frequently found it necessary to supply their food from the countryside. Blacks played a very decisive role in assisting General William T. Sherman in his "march to the sea." Sherman's success in feeding over sixty-five thousand troops while on the march in enemy country was one of the most remarkable feats in history; without the help of the blacks this would have been impossible.

Throughout the war southern blacks rendered valuable assistance to northern soldiers who escaped from Confederate prisons and were trying to find their way back to Union lines. Many prisoners stated that it would have been impossible for them to have reached Union lines without the aid of the blacks.

Black women and men behind the lines contributed to the war effort by serving as nurses and aides in caring for the sick and wounded. Harriet Tubman, Susie King Taylor, and Sojourner Truth were among the prominent black nurses who served in the Union camps and hospitals. Blacks were cooks, servants, and laundresses in the Union hospitals. Black nurses, aides, and missionaries served also in contraband camps.

Blacks were active in the organization of schools for freedmen. Southern state laws had made it a crime to teach blacks to read and write. The first contraband school in the South was started by Mary Chase, a freedwoman of Alexandria, Virginia, on 1 September 1861. In subsequent months, missionary associations (both black and white), churches, and black individuals established schools throughout the South and in some northern cities for the freedmen. Mrs. Mary S. Peake, a black woman, became one of the most prominent teachers for the American Missionary Association at Hampton, Virginia. Charlotte L. Forten and Susie King Taylor were also outstanding black teachers in the South with the Union army. Many other blacks served as teachers with the Freedmen's Bureau in the South. The people and organizations responsible for establishing these schools and teaching the blacks the rudiments of education made a most significant contribution to the adjustment of blacks coming out of slavery.

In every northern city with a sizable black population the black churches and secular leaders formed freedmen's aid associations. As early as February 1862, meetings were held in many northern cities for the express purpose of rendering aid to the blacks in the South. Within months many relief associations were organized. Mrs. Elizabeth Keckley, Mrs. Lincoln's black seamstress, was the organizer of the well known Contraband Relief Association of Washington. These associations solicited gifts of clothing and donations of cash. They distributed hundreds of barrels and boxes of donated clothing as well as food and medical supplies to needy contrabands.

The Civil War accelerated black Americans' drive for civil rights and desegregation in the North. Discrimination against blacks and the firmly held belief in the superiority of the white race were not restricted to the South but were shared by an overwhelming majority of white Americans in the North. In most parts of the North in 1861, black men did not enjoy equal rights.

Blacks could vote on equal terms with whites in only five states: Maine, Hew Hampshire, Vermont, Massachusetts, and Rhode Island. These states contained only seven percent of the northern population. Several states prohibited blacks from testifying against whites in court. Public accommodations, transportation facilities, restuarants, hotels, and theaters in some parts of the North were segregated. Blacks were barred from jury service in every state except Massachusetts. Public schools in most of the northern cities were segregated. Blacks also suffered discrimination in housing and jobs in every part of the North.

The most eloquent and persistent spokesman for racial equality during the war was Frederick Douglass. He lectured all over the North in behalf of emancipation and equal rights. His lectures drew large crowds and his monthly journal was read by many. Douglass had several meetings with President Lincoln during the war to discuss slavery, enlistment of blacks in the Union army, discrimination against black soldiers, civil rights for blacks, and other issues related to blacks. Some of the more important gains for civil rights for blacks during the war were made on the national level. Under the leadership of Charles Sumner, Congress passed several antidiscrimination measures. Legal barriers fell rapidly in most parts of the North during or immediately after the Civil War, but other forms of discrimination proved more resistent.

This study demonstrates that the exclusion of blacks from the Union army worked only so long as the government and northern whites remained confident of their ability to win the war. But as the months passed and the expected victory over the South did not materialize, the frustrated Union was forced to consider emancipation and black recruitment. Although many of the more than two hundred thousand black soldiers and sailors who served in the Union army and navy came from the cities, most of them were fugitives or recently emancipated slaves from southern plantations. Thomas W. Higginson stated that, "till the blacks are armed, there was no guaranty of their freedom. It was their demeanor under arms that shamed the nation into recognizing them as men."[2] Black Americans in the Union army and navy proved their manhood and established a strong claim to equality of treatment and opportunity.

It is hoped that in the future the history of the American Civil War will be presented as it happened as the combined effort of

Americans--black and white--who worked, fought, and died together to save the Union. It is the author's opinion that the denial of equal justice and full equality to American blacks has been due in part to the consistent distortions and myths about their role in the past. The writer further believes that many black students have been "turned off" from studying American history and in some cases "turned off" from school altogether by the way their history texts and teachers presented American history with respect to the role of black Americans. This book and the teaching unit that follows are attempts to put black Americans in their appropriate place in a typical unit taught on the Civil War in a secondary or college survey American history course.

CHAPTER VI

TEACHING UNIT ON BLACK AMERICANS AND THEIR CONTRIBUTIONS TOWARD UNION VICTORY IN THE CIVIL WAR, 1861-1865

The central focus of this chapter is to demonstrate how black Americans and their contributions toward Union victory in the American Civil War may be integrated into a teaching unit in secondary and college survey history courses. This teaching unit is not designed for courses in black history.

As a result of the civil rights movement of the 1960s many dramatic changes took place in the status of black Americans. Across the nation blacks' presence became more visible in sports, entertainment, politics, education, and in practically all other areas. But it was in the massive slums of American cities that blacks became more visible to white Americans. For here, the black masses revolted against poverty and their state of helplessness. The militancy and violence were seen by middle-class white Americans as a threat to their security. Many white Americans were unable to understand why blacks were not satisfied with their status. In an attempt to resolve this problem, attention began to focus on black history as a guide in helping public authorities make policy. Because of myths, distortions, and omissions that surrounded black Americans' past, students (black and white) began to demand that more emphasis be placed on the history of black Americans. At first there were only a few schools outside of the black colleges and universities that taught black history. As a result, many schools began to establish Black Studies courses and programs. Many students argued that without these courses they would be ignorant of their origins and past.

The author believes there would be little need for black history courses if the textbooks and instructors of American history integrated the role and contributions of black Americans into each unit. The author further believes that the observance of Black History Week or Month each February is not sufficient to point out the many contributions of black Americans and the role they played in our history. Furthermore, to reduce the contributions of black Americans to the attention of the students and laymen to one week or even one month of the year in itself is a mockery of black

American's accomplishments. It also segregates black Americans' past from that of white Americans. It is hoped that the preceding pages of this book, as well as this teaching unit and the bibliography that follows, will give the classroom teacher the basic tools necessary for the integration of black Americans and their contributions into a traditional teaching unit on the Civil War.

This unit is patterned after one that is generally used in secondary school and college survey American history courses. The instructor can easily integrate the role and contributions of the blacks into each topic of the traditional unit. The time allowed for the completion of this unit is approximately two to three weeks. This unit is not meant to be completely exhaustive. The materials selected by the teacher would depend on the reading levels of the students.

Finally, there is no special methodology to be used in integrating this supplementary unit into a traditional unit on the Civil War. The teacher should use any methods that he or she has successfully employed in the past--outside reading assignments, class discussions, dramatizations, lectures, assigned homework, research projects, charts, movies, bulletin board displays, filmstrips, etc. The methodology will vary from teacher to teacher and from class to class. However, regardless of the methodology, the teacher should continue to focus on the basic goal of presenting American history in such a way as to instill a pride in the black students of their American heritage and to instill in other students an understanding of black Americans' contributions to the nation.

In integrating this unit into the traditional unit, the teacher should keep these objectives in mind:

1. To demonstrate that black Americans never willingly accepted slavery or second-class citizenship but battled in valiant and practical ways to achieve the promise of America.

2. To show that black Americans and their role in our history must be seen in the context of the larger picture of American growth and problems.

3. To demonstrate that black Americans' contributions to Union victory in the American Civil War were made despite the most adverse conditions.

114

4. To demonstrate that the Civil War resulted in a revolution in the status of blacks, North as well as South. It brought freedom, citizenship, and, eventually, equal civil and political rights (in theory at least) to all black Americans.

The following outline offers a suggested framework for the full-scale integration of black Americans and their contributions into a traditional teaching unit on the American Civil War.

I. Introduction
   A. Status of Black Americans, North and South, in 1860
   B. The Presidential Election of 1860
      1. Northern black support of Abraham Lincoln
      2. Reaction of northern blacks to the Crittenden Compromise
      3. The formation of the Confederate States of America

II. The Outbreak of War
   A. Fall of Fort Sumter
   B. Lincoln's Call to Arms
      1. Black Americans' response
      2. Reasons for rejection of black enlistment
   C. Northern Blacks in Noncombatant Positions
      1. Cooks, servants, teamsters, and laborers
   D. Blacks Join Union Navy
   E. Strengths and Weaknesses of Both Sides
   F. Military Strategy of Both Sides at the Outset of War

III. Changing Union Policy Toward the Employment of Blacks
   A. Deserting Slaves to Union Lines
   B. General Butler's Contraband Policy
   C. Frederick Douglass and Other Abolitionists Urge Emancipation and Employment of Blacks as Soldiers
   D. Contraband Camps
   E. Unofficial Black Soldiers in the Union Army
   F. Lincoln's Position on Slavery and Black Soldiers in 1861-62

IV. Early Military Campaigns, 1861-62
   A. Battle of Bull Run and Results
   B. Union Victories Along the Confederate Coasts
      1. <u>Monitor</u> v. <u>Merrimac</u>

115

        a. Mary Louvestre
        b. Results of Union blockade
     2. Black Americans in the Union Navy
        a. Robert Smalls
        b. William Tillman
        c. Jacob Garrick
        d. Aaron Anderson
        e. Robert Blake
        f. John Lawson
        g. Joachim Pease
  C. Western Campaigns
  D. Second Bull Run
     1. Mounting Union casualities, desertions,
        difficulty in obtaining enlistments
     2. Enemy slaves represent a source of strength
  E. Battle of Antietam
     1. McClellan removed
     2. Preliminary Emancipation Proclamation

V.   The Emancipation Proclamation
  A. Why Lincoln Issued the Proclamation
  B. Results of the Emancipation Proclamation
     1. Blacks officially enlist in Union army
     2. Northern riots against conscription of blacks
     3. Southern and foreign reaction to the proclamation
  C. Conditions Under Which Black Soldiers Fought
     1. Received less training than whites
     2. Received half the pay given white soldiers for
        the first eighteen months after officially enlisted
     3. Received poorer medical care
     4. Commanded by white officers
     5. Not treated as prisoners of war when captured by
        the enemy
     6. Unrepresented in court-martial proceedings and
        excluded from military academies
     7. Disproportionate number of blacks often assigned
        to heavy labor and fatigue duty

VI. Black Soldiers in the Union Army
  A. Battles of Port Hudson, Milliken's Bend, Fort
     Wagner, Moscow, Olustee, Chancellorsville
  B. Blacks in the Virginia Theater
  C. Total Black Involvement

D. The Collapse of the Confederacy

E. Lincoln's Assassination and Black Americans' Reaction

VII. Blacks Behind the Union Lines

A. Blacks as Union Spies, Nurses, Laborers, Servants, Cooks, Etc.

B. Labor Problems Relating to the Blacks in the North

C. Blacks as Leaders in the Following:
1. Recruitment of black soldiers and demand for their acceptance in the Union army
2. Pressure for equal treatment of black soldiers after enlistment
3. Pressure on Congress and the President for the abolition of slavery
4. Demand for full equality for all blacks, North and South

D. Northern Blacks' Aid to Ex-slaves
1. Organization of schools and relief agencies
2. Work in contraband camps as teachers and nurses
3. Work in Freedmen's Bureau

The following is a suggested list of persons for individual or committee reports:

Robert Smalls	Charlotte Forten
Thomas W. Higginson	Mary Louvestre
William Lloyd Garrison	John Scobell
Elizabeth Van Lew	Mary Elizabeth Bowser
Harriet Tubman	Henry Blake
Frederick Douglass	Susie King Taylor
Sojourner Truth	Mary S. Peake
Martin R. Delany	Elizabeth Keckley
Wendell Phillips	

The following sources are recommended for this unit. The books suggested, however, do not represent an exhaustive list. Rather, the purpose of these suggestions is to provide the teachers and students with a good general knowledge of the role and contributions of black Americans during the Civil War.

1. James M. McPherson, The Negro's Civil War: How American Negroes Felt and Acted During the War for the Union (New York: Random House, 1965) presents a fascinating picture

of what black Americans said and did during the war through eyewitness accounts tied together by important editorial comments and factual information. Recommended for teachers and college students. The Struggle for Equality: Abolitionists and the Negro in the Civil War and Reconstruction (Princeton: Princeton University Press, 1968) is another excellent book by McPherson. Recommended for all levels (high school, college, teachers).

2. Dudley T. Cornish, The Sable Arm: Negro Troops in the Union Army (New York: W. W. Norton & Co., 1966) is a full story of black troops in the Union army. Recommended for all levels.

3. Lerone Bennett, Jr., Before the Mayflower (New York: Penguin Books, 1981). Chapter VII details the black man's part in the Civil War. Recommended as reference reading by teachers or as supplementary or research reading by students of all levels.

4. Thomas Wentworth Higginson, Army Life in a Black Regiment (Williamstown, Mass.: Corner House Publishers, 1870; reprinted 1971) is the story of the first official black regiment of the Civil War, told by their commander, an ardent abolitionist. Recommended for all levels.

5. Rayford W. Logan and Irving S. Cohen, The American Negro (Boston: Houghton Mifflin, 1967). Chapter V relates the part played by black Americans in the Civil War. Recommended for supplementary reading or research by students of all levels.

6. Ray Allen Billington, ed., The Journal of Charlotte Forten: A Free Negro in the Slave Era (New York: The Macmillan Co., 1967) details a young black teacher's role in instructing former slaves in the Georgia Sea Islands during the war, a realistic picture of black self-help at this time. This book should appeal to all levels.

7. Dorothy Sterling, Freedom Train (New York: Doubleday, 1954), pages 136-177 describe heroine Harriet Tubman's labor for the Union army during the war. Recommended for high school students. Sarah Bradford, Harriet Tubman: The Moses of Her People (Secaucus, New Jersey: The Citadel Press, 1974) is also an excellent work on Tubman and should appeal to all levels.

8. Dorothy Sterling, Captain of the Planter (New York: Doubleday, 1958) is the story of Robert Smalls, the black pilot who delivered his Confederate gunboat to the Union navy and later served five terms as a South Carolina congressman. It is well written, has excellent pictures, and is carefully researched. Excellent reading for high school students.

9. John Hope Franklin, From Slavery to Freedom (New York: Vintage Books, 1969) is the most complete history of black Americans. Chapter XVI deals with the Civil War and the role of black Americans. The Emancipation Proclamation (New York: Doubleday, 1965) is another work of Franklin which details the background events and meaning of the first presidential order to affect American blacks. Should appeal to all levels.

10. William Loren Katz, Eyewitness: The Negro in American History (New York: Pitman, 1971). Chapter IX discusses the black man's part in the Civil War through text, pictures, and eyewitness accounts. An excellent book and should appeal to all levels.

11. Susie King Taylor, Reminiscences of My Life in Camp (New York: Arno Press, 1968) is a reprint of the autobiography of a black Civil War nurse. Recommended as outside reading for students of all levels.

12. Irvin H. Lee, Negro Medal of Honor Man (New York: Dodd & Mead), 1967). Chapter III is the story of twenty blacks who won the Medal of Honor during the Civil War. Recommended for high school readers.

13. Benjamin Quarles has three excellent books for this unit. The Negro in the Making of America (New York: Collier, 1964) is a popular history of black Americans. It is organized according to the main chronological periods of our history and combines much valuable information with an adroit writing style. The Negro in the Civil War (Boston: Little, Brown, & Co., 1969) and Black Abolitionists (New York: Oxford University, 1969) are scholarly studies of the role of black Americans during the Civil War.

14. There are several works on Frederick Douglass (Boston: Little Brown & Co., 1980); Benjamin Quarles, Frederick Douglass (New York: Atheneum, 1969); and Shirley Graham, There was Once a Slave: The Heroic Story of Frederick Douglass (New York:

Julian Messner, Inc., 1947). These books should appeal to all levels.

Some teachers have found that classroom use of appropriate films and filmstrips often serves to increase student interest as well as to stimulate class discussions.

The following is a list of films and filmstrips applicable to this unit.

1. Harriet Tubman and the Underground Railroad. 21 min. (black and white). A portrayal of the former slave who became one of the most daring conductors of the underground railroad that carried fugitive slaves to freedom.
> McGraw-Hill Films
> 110 15th Street
> Delma, California 92014

2. Civil War and Reconstruction, 1861-1877. 20 min. (black and white). Covers the Negro role in the war and the attempt at reconstruction that followed. Its pictures are excellent, the text is terse and exciting. Most useful as an overview of the period. This documentary should have appeal for senior high students.
> McGraw-Hill Films

3. The Negro in the Civil War and Reconstruction. Filmstrip—color. Covers the same topics as the film above but allows the teacher more time for depth treatment of the various topics.
> McGraw-Hill Films

4. The Civil War: Anguish of Emancipation. 20. min. A reenactment of the steps toward Lincoln's issuing of the Proclamation using verbatim dialogue.
> Learning Corporation of America
> 1350 Avenue of the Americas
> New York, New York 10019

5. The Civil War: Promise of Reconstruction. 28 min. A reenactment of the Port Royal experiment and the related problems for blacks and whites.
> Learning Corporation of America

6. The History of the Black Man in the United States. Set of sound filmstrips. This correlated sound filmstrip color set offers

a broad survey of the experience of the black people of the United States from Colonial times to the present. While emphasis is placed on events as they affected black people these events are set against the background of the general conditions in the United States in each period of history. Parts 1 and 2 are applicable to this unit.

Educational Audio Visual Inc.
Pleasantville, New York 10570

Afro-American History Posters (New York: Pitman Co.) is an attractive collection of fifteen posters showing how blacks have contributed to important aspects of American history. Four of these posters cover blacks in the Civil War.

The stated objectives for this supplementary unit may be evaluated by traditional methods of testing, such as written essay and objective questions, as well as oral examinations.

APPENDIX A

A LIST OF SIGNIFICANT CIVIL WAR BATTLES
ENGAGED IN BY BLACK TROOPS

Amite River
Appomattox Court
   House
Arkansas River
Ash Bayou
Ashepoo River
Ashwood Landing
Athens
Barrancas
Bayou Bidell
Bayou Boeuf
Bayou Macon
Bayou St. Lewis
Bayou Tensas
Bayou Tunica
Bermuda Hundreds
Berwick
Big Creek
Big River
Big Springs
Black Creek
Black River
Boggs' Mill
Boyd's Station
Boykin's Mills
Bradford Spring
Brawley Fork
Brice's Cross Roads
Brigsen Creek
Brush Creek
Bryant's Plantation
Cabin Creek
Cabin Point
Camden
Cedar Keys
Chaffin's Farm
Charleston
Chattanooga

City Point
Clarkesville
Clinton
Coleman's
   Plantation
Columbia
Concordia Bayou
Cow Creek
Cox's Bridge
Dallas
Dalton
Darbytown Road
David's Bend
Decatur
Deep Bottom
Deveraux Neck
Drewry's Bluff
Dutch Gap
East Pascagoula
Eastport
Fair Oaks
Federal Point
Fillmore
Floyd
Fort Adams
Fort Anderson
Fort Blakely
Fort Brady
Fort Burnham
Fort Donelson
Fort Gaines
Fort Gibson
Fort Jones
Fort Pillow
Fort Pocahontas
Fort Smith
Fort Taylor
Fort Wagner

Franklin
Ghent
Glasgow
Goodrich's Landing
Grand Gulf
Gregory's Farm
Haines' Bluff
Hall Island
Harrodsburg
Hatcher's Run
Helena
Henderson
Holly Springs
Honey Hill
Hopkinsville
Horsehead Creek
Indian Bay
Indian Town
Indian Village
Island Mound
Island No. 76
Issequena County
Jackson
Jacksonville
James Island
Jenkin's Ferry
John's Island
Johnsonville
Jones' Bridge
Joy's Ford
Lake Prividence
Laurence
Little Rock
Liverpool Heights
Madison Station
Magnolia
Marengo
Mariana

123

Marion	Point of Rocks	Steamer Chippewa
Marion County	Point Pleasant	Steamer City Belle
McKay's Point	Poison Springs	Steamer Louts
Meffleton Lodge	Port Hudson	Suffolk
Memphis	Powhatan	Sugar Loaf Hill
Milliken's Bend	Prairie d' Anne	Sulphur Branch
Milltown Bluff	Pulaski	Swift Creek
Mitchell's Creek	Raleigh	Taylorsville
Morganzia	Rector's Farm	Timber Hill
Moscow Station	Richland	Town Creek
Mound Plantation	Richmond	Township
Mound Pleasant	Ripley	Trestle
Landing	Roache's Plantation	Tupelo
Mud Creek	Rolling Fork	Vicksburg
Murfreesboro	Rooseville Creek	Vidalia
Nashville	Ross Landing	Wallace Ferry
Natchez	Sabine River	Warsaw
Natural Bridge	Salkehatchie	Waterford
New Kent Court House	Saltville	Waterloo
New Market Heights	Sand Mountain	Waterproof
Olustee	Sandy Swamp	White Oak Road
Owensboro	Scottsboro	White River
Pass Manchal	Sherwood	Williamsburg
Palmetto Ranch	Shipwith's Landing	Wilmington
Pettersburg	Simpsonville	Wilson's Landing, Wharf
Pierson's Farm	Smithfield	Yazoo City
Pine Barren Creek	South Tunnel	Yazoo Expedition
Pine Barren Ford	Spanish Fort	
Pine Bluff	St. John's River	
Plymouth	St. Stephens	
Point Lookout	Steamer Alliance	

Source: Harry A. Ploski and Warren Marr, II, The Negro Almanac: A Reference Work on the Afro-American (New York: The Bellwether Co., 1976), p. 615.

APPENDIX B

BLACK SERVICEMEN AWARDED THE CONGRESSIONAL MEDAL OF HONOR

William Appleton
4th U.S. Colored Troops, September 29, 1864, for gallant conduct at New Market Heights, Virginia.

Private William H. Barnes
38th U.S. Colored Troops, among the first to enter the Confederate works, although wounded, at Chaffin's Farm near Richmond, Virginia.

First Sergeant Powhatan Beaty
5th U.S. Colored Troops, September 29, 1864, gallantry in action at Chaffin's Farm near Richmond.

First Sergeant James H. Bronson
5th U.S. Colored Troops, September 29, 1864, gallantry in action at Chaffin's Farm near Richmond.

Sergeant William H. Carney
54th Massachusetts Colored Infantry, the first black to win the Congressional Medal of Honor. Carney was cited for valor on June 18, 1863, during the Battle of Fort Wagner, South Carolina, in which he carried the colors, and led a charge to the parapet after the standard bearer had been killed. He was twice severly wounded during this battle.

Sergeant Decatur Dorsey
39th U.S. Colored Troops. Dorsey was cited for valor in the Battle of Petersburg, Virginia, on July 30, 1864. When his regiment was driven back to Union lines, he carried the colors and rallied the men in his unit.

Sergeant-Major Christian A. Fleetwood
4th U.S. Colored Troops, for gallantry in action at Chaffin's farm near Richmond.

Private James Gardiner
36th U.S. Colored Troops, cited for gallantry in action at Chaffin's Farm near Richmond.

Sergeant James H. Harris
38th Colored Troops, cited for gallantry in action at Chaffin's Farm near Richmond.

Sergeant-Major Thomas Hawkins
6th U.S. Colored Troops, cited for valor in the Battle of Deep Bottom, Virginia, on July 21, 1864. He was credited with the rescue of his regimental colors from the enemy.

Sergeant Alfred B. Hilton
4th U.S. Colored Troops, cited for gallantry in action at Chaffin's Farm near Richmond.

Sergeant-Major Milton M. Holland
5th U.S. Colored Troops, cited for gallantry in action at Chaffin's Farm near Richmond.

Corporal Miles James
36th U.S. Colored Troops, cited for gallantry in action at Chaffin's Farm near Richmond.

First Sergeant Alexander Kelly
6th U.S. Colored Troops, cited for gallantry in action at Chaffin's Farm near Richmond.

First Sergeant Robert Pinn
5th U.S. Colored Troops, cited for gallant conduct in action at Chaffin's Farm near Richmond.

First Sergeant Edward Radcliff
38th U.S. Troops, cited for gallantry in action at Chaffin's Farm near Richmond.

Private Charles Veal
4th U.S. Colored Troops, cited for gallantry in action at Chaffin's Farm near Richmond.

U.S. NAVY

Aaron Anderson
Participated in the clearing of Mattox Creek on March 17, 1865, while serving on the gunboat _Wyandank_. Anderson was cited for carrying out his duties courageously in spite of devastating fire from the enemy.

Robert Blake
Was an ex-slave, enlisting in the navy after escaping from a Virginia plantation. Blake displayed heroism while serving on the gunboat Marblehead on December 25, 1863.

John Lawson
Was awarded the medal for his bravery at the Battle of Mobile Bay while serving on the gunboat Hartford on August 5, 1864. Lawson was knocked unconscious during the battle, but as soon as he regained consciousness he zealously continued to perform his duties, although four of the men at his station had been killed by enemy fire.

Joachim Pease
Was awarded the medal for gallantry in action while serving on the gunboat Kearsarge in its famed engagement with the Confederate Alabama.

Sources: Harry A. Ploski and Warren Marr, II, The Negro Almanac: A Reference Work on the Afro-American (New York: The Bellwether Co., 1976), pp. 642-43, 646-47; Benjamin Quarles, The Negro in the Civil War (Boston: Little, Brown & Co., 1969), pp. 231-32.

BLACK SOLDIERS ACCREDITED TO EACH STATE
DURING THE CIVIL WAR

According to the statistics on file in the Adjutant General's office, the states were accredited with the following number of blacks who served in the army during the Civil War.

Alabama	2,969	Vermont	120
Louisiana	24,052	Rhode Island	1,837
New Hampshire	125	New York	4,125
Massachusetts	3,966	Pennsylvania	8,612
Connecticut	1,764	Maryland	8,718
New Jersey	1,185	Virginia	5,723
Delaware	954	West Virginia	196
District of Columbia	3,269	Georgia	3,486
North Carolina	5,035	Arkansas	5,526
South Carolina	5,462	Kentucky	23,703
Florida	1,044	Ohio	5,092
Tennessee	20,133	Illinois	1,811
Michigan	1,387	Minnesota	104
Indiana	1,537	Wisconsin	104
Missouri	8,344	Texas	47
Iowa	440		
Kansas	2,080	Not accounted for	5,896
Colorado Territory	95	Total	178,975
Mississippi	17,896		
Maine	104		

The losses these troops sustained from sickness, wounds, killed in battle, and other casualties incident to war were 68,178. The aggregate black population in the United States in 1860 was 4,449,201, of which 3,950,531 were slaves.

Source: Joseph T. Wilson, The Black Phalanx: A History of the Negro Soldiers of the United States in the Wars of 1775-1812, 1861-65 (Hartford: American Publishing Co., 1890; reprint ed., New York: Arno Press, 1968), p. 142.

CHAPTER I

[1]Benjamin Quarles, The Negro in the Civil War (Boston: Little, Brown & Co., 1969), pp. 22-25; George W. Williams, A History of the Negro Troops in the War of the Rebellion, 1861-65 (New York: Harper & Brothers, 1888; reprint ed., New York: Negro Universities Press, 1969), p. 65.

[2]James H. McPherson, The Negro's Civil War: How American Negroes Felt and Acted During the War for the Union (New York: Random House, 1965), pp. 19-36; Herbert Aptheker, A Documentary History of the Negro People in the United States, 2 vols. (New York: The Citadel Press, 1968), 1:459-71.

[3]Philip S. Foner, The Life and Writings of Frederick Douglass: The Civil War 1861-1865, 4 vols. (New York: International Publishers, 1952), 3:12-14; Shirley Graham, There was Once a Slave: The Heroic Story of Frederick Douglass (New York: Julian Messner, Inc., 1947), pp. 219-22; Nathan Irvin Huggins, Slave and Citizen: The Life of Frederick Douglass (Boston: Little, Brown & Co., 1980), pp. 76-77.

[4]John Hope Franklin, From Slavery to Freedom: A History of Negro Americans (New York: Random House, 1969), p. 272; McPherson, The Negro's Civil War, pp. 19-23.

[5]The War of the Rebellion: Official Records of the Union and Confederate Armies, 128 vols. (Washington: Government Printing Office, 1880-1902), Series 3, Vol. I, pp. 107, 133.

[6]Quarles, The Negro in the Civil War, p. 30; Foner, The Life and Writings of Frederick Douglass, 3:18.

[7]Benjamin Quarles, Lincoln and the Negro (New York: Oxford University Press, 1962), pp. 67-68.

[8]Stephen B. Oates, With Malice Toward None: The Life of Abraham Lincoln (New York: Harper & Row, Publishers, 1977), pp. 236-37.

[9]Leon F. Litwack, Been in the Storm So Long: The Aftermath of Slavery (New York: Alfred A. Knopf, Inc., 1979), p. 66; McPherson, The Negro's Civil War, pp. 99-100; Williams, A History of the Negro Troops in the War of the Rebellion, pp. 170-73.

[10]Joseph T. Wilson, The Black Phalanx: A History of the Negro Soldiers of the United States in the Wars of 1775-1812, 1861-1865 (Hartford: American Publishing Co., 1890; reprint ed., New York: Arno Press, 1968), pp. 93-110; Litwack, Been in the Storm So Long, p. 66.

[11]Merton L. Dillon, The Abolitionists: The Growth of a Dissenting Minority (New York: W. W. Norton & Co., 1979), pp. 251-55; James M. McPherson, The Struggle for Equality: Abolitionists and the Negro in the Civil War and Reconstruction (Princeton: Princeton University Press, 1968), p. 134.

[12]Foner, The Life and Writings of Frederick Douglass, 3:152-54. For an excellent study of the Confederate blacks, see James H. Brewer, The Confederate Negro: Virginia's Craftsmen and Military Laborers, 1861-1865 (Durham, N.C.: Duke University Press, 1969); Bobby Lee Lovett also discusses the Confederate black Tennesseans in his Ph.D. dissertation, "The Negro in Tennessee, 1861-1866: A Socio-Military History of the Civil War Era" (Ph.D. dissertation, University of Arkansas, 1978), pp. 6-12.

[13]McPherson, The Struggle for Equality, pp. 141-42.

[14]Quarles, Negro in the Civil War, pp. 141-42.

[15]James L. Roark, Masters Without Slaves: Southern Planters in the Civil War and Reconstruction (New York: W. W. Norton & Co., 1977), pp. 70-73; McPherson, Negro's Civil War, p. 24. For an excellent study of the status of free blacks in Tennessee, see Roger Raymond Van Dyke's Ph.D. dissertation, "The Free Negro in Tennessee, 1790-1860" (Ph.D. dissertation, Florida State University, 1972). William L. Imes also discusses the status of free blacks in Tennessee in his article, "The Legal Status of Free Negroes and Slaves in Tennessee," Journal of Negro History 4 (1919): 254-73.

[16]Roark, Masters Without Slaves, pp. 74-76; John W. Blassingame, Black New Orleans, 1860-1880 (Chicago: The University of Chicago Press, 1973), p. 25.

[17]Quarles, Negro in the Civil War, pp. 43-47.

[18]Litwack, Been in the Storm So Long, pp. 106-114.

[19]Carl Sandburg, Abraham Lincoln: The War Years, 4 vols. (New York: Harcourt, Brace & World, Inc., 1939), 1:293-94.

[20]Official Records, Series 2, Vol. I, p. 752; Sister Elizabeth Allen, "Women Missionaries and the Education of the Blacks in Hampton, Virginia, 1861-1868" (Master's thesis, Middle Tennessee State University, 1977), pp. 2-3; William L. Katz, Eyewitness: The Negro in American History (New York: Pittman Publishing Corporation, 1971), pp. 210-11.

[21]Hans L. Trefousse, Ben Butler: The South Called Him Beast (New York: Octagon Books, 1974), p. 79; Allen, "Women Missionaries," p. 3.

[22]Trefousse, Ben Butler, p. 79; Allen, "Women Missionaries," p. 4; Katz, Eyewitness, pp. 210-11; Dudley T. Cornish, The Sable Arm: Negro Troops in the Union Army, 1861-1865 (New York: W. W. Norton & Co., 1966), p. 24.

[23]Louis S. Gerteis, From Contraband to Freedman: Federal Policy Toward Southern Blacks (Westport, Conn.: Greenwood Press, Inc., 1973), pp. 15-18; Allen, "Women Missionaries," pp. 4-5; McPherson, The Struggle for Equality, p. 156.

[24]Allen, "Women Missionaries," pp. 4-5.

[25]Trefousse, Ben Butler, pp. 77-97; McPherson, The Struggle for Equality, pp. 156-57; Gerteis, From Contraband to Freedman, pp. 18-19.

[26]Quarles, Negro in the Civil War, pp. 61-62.

[27]Ibid., pp. 56-62. For an interesting discussion on the reactions of those blacks who remained on the plantations to the arrival of the Union soldiers, see Chapter 3 in Litwack, Been in the Storm So Long, pp. 104-66.

[28]Trefousse, Ben Butler, p. 78; Katz, Eyewitness, pp. 208-209.

[29]Sandburg, Lincoln, 1:556-57; Official Records, Series 2, Vol. I, pp. 759, 762-63.

[30]Ferol Egan, Fremont: Explorer for a Restless Nation (New York: Doubleday & Co., Inc., 1977), p. 515; Huggins, Slave and Citizen, p. 79; Quarles, Negro in the Civil War, pp. 66-67; Robert Cruden, The War that Never Ended: The American Civil War (Englewood Cliffs, New Jersey: Prentice-Hall, Inc., 1973, p. 134.

[31]Egan, Fremont, pp. 515-18; Oates, With Malice Toward None, pp. 260-62; Cruden, The War that Never Ended, p. 134.

[32]Roy P. Basler, ed., The Collected Works of Abraham Lincoln, 9 vols. (New Brunswick, New Jersey, 1953), 5:48-49; Cruden, The War that Never Ended, pp. 134-35.

[33]Huggins, Slave and Citizen, p. 80; Benjamin Quarles, Frederick Douglass (New York: Atheneum, 1969), pp. 191-92.

[34]Official Records, Series 2, Vol. I, pp. 770-71.

[35]Ibid., pp. 774-75.

[36]Ibid., Series 1, Vol. XVIII, pp. 369, 461; Lovett, "The Negro in Tennessee," pp. 14-20.

[37]Allen, "Women Missionaries," pp. 6-8; Lovett, "The Negro in Tennessee," pp. 17-20; McPherson, Negro's Civil War, pp. 133-35; Cam Walker, "Corinth, the Story of a Contraband Camp," Civil War History 20 (1974): 5-22.

[38]Official Records, Series 3, Vol. II, pp. 27-28; John G. Sproat, "Blueprint for Radical Reconstruction," Journal of Southern History 23 (February 1957): 25-32.

[39]George R. Bentley, A History of the Freedmen's Bureau (New York: Octagon Books, 1974), pp. 24-25.

[40]Ibid., pp. 24-26; Gerteis, From Contraband to Freedman, pp. 53-55. Chapter IV of this book discusses further the conflict between the War and Treasury Departments concerning authority over the freedmen and abandoned lands.

[41]Willie L. Rose, Rehearsal for Reconstruction: The Port Royal Experiment (New York: Oxford University Press, 1964), pp. 11-16; Gerteis, From Contraband to Freedman, pp. 50-58; McPherson, Negro's Civil War, pp. 113-22.

[42]Official Records, Series 3, Vol. II, p. 55; Rose, Rehearsal for Reconstruction, pp. 18-31; Gerteis, From Contraband to Freedman, pp. 51-52.

[43]Official Records, Series 2, Vol. I, p. 802; Bentley, History of the Freedmen's Bureau, pp. 7-10; McPherson, Struggle for Equality, p. 165.

[44]Sandburg, Lincoln, 1:562-63; Roy P. Basler, Lincoln (New York: Octagon Books, 1975), 5:118-19; Oates, With Malice Toward None, pp. 325-26; W. M. Brewer, "Lincoln and the Border States," Journal of Negro History 34 (January 1949): 59-60.

[45]Quarles, Negro in the Civil War, pp. 136-38.

[46]Van Dyke, "The Free Negro in Tennessee," pp. 175-79; Sandburg, Lincoln, 1:574-77; Paul J. Scheips, "Lincoln and the

Chiriqui Colonization Project," Journal of Negro History 37 (October 1952): 418-22.

[47]Van Dyke, "The Free Negro in Tennessee," pp. 175-79; McPherson, Negro's Civil War, pp. 77-97.

[48]Basler, Works of Lincoln, 5:370-75; Sandburg, Lincoln, 1:574-76; Scheips, "Lincoln and the Colonization Project," pp. 423-24.

[49]McPherson, Struggle for Equality, p. 155; Huggins, Slave and Citizen, pp. 82-84; Scheips, "Lincoln and the Colonization Project," pp. 423-24.

[50]Aptheker, A Documentary History of the Negro, 1:471-75; Quarles, Douglass, pp. 194-97; Sandburg, Lincoln, 1:577-79

[51]McPherson, Negro's Civil War, pp. 164-65.

[52]Official Records, Series 3, Vol. II, pp. 29-31, 42, 54, 57, 147, 196-98, 292, 246; Series 1, Vol. XIV, p. 341; Sandburg, Lincoln, 1:561-62; Basler, Lincoln, 5:121-22.

[53]Trefousse, Ben Butler, pp. 130-31; McPherson, Negro's Civil War, pp. 160-65.

[54]Official Records, Series 3, Vol. V, pp. 657-58; Litwack, Been in the Storm So Long, pp. 68-69.

[55]Thomas W. Higginson, Army Life in a Black Regiment (Williamstown, Mass.: Corner House Publishers, 1870; reprinted 1971), pp. 2-5; Official Records, Series 1, Vol. XIV, pp. 377-78; Litwack, Been in the Storm So Long, p. 68.

[56]Official Records, Series 1, Vol. XIV, pp. 194-98; Higginson, Army Life in a Black Regiment, pp. 2-5.

[57]McPherson, Struggle for Equality, p. 200.

[58]Higginson, Army Life in a Black Regiment, pp. 243-63.

[59]Quarles, Negro in the Civil War, pp. 118-20.

[60]Official Records, Series 3, Vol. II, pp. 436-38; Vol. XV, pp. 556-57.

[61]Cornish, The Sable Arm, p. 67; Williams, Negro Troops in the War of the Rebellion, pp. 98-99.

[62]Sandburg, Lincoln, 1:582-84; Oates, With Malice Toward None, pp. 317-19; Basler, Lincoln, 5:126-30.

[63]Sandburg, Lincoln, 1:586-88; Oates, With Malice Toward None, pp. 320-23.

[64]Hans L. Trefousse, Lincoln's Decision for Emancipation (New York: J. B. Lippincott Co., 1975), pp. 28-49;

McPherson, Struggle for Equality, pp. 117-20; Quarles, Douglass, pp. 198-202.

[65]Trefousse, Lincoln's Decision for Emancipation, pp. 48-49; McPherson, Struggle for Equality, p. 120; Oates, With Malice Toward None, pp. 330-31.

[66]John Hope Franklin, The Emancipation Proclamation (Garden City, New York: Doubleday & Co., Inc., 1965), p. 89; Cruden, The War that Never Ended, p. 138; Oates, With Malice Toward None, pp. 332-33.

[67]Quarles, Negro in the Civil War, pp. 183-99.

[68]McPherson, Negro's Civil War, pp. 160-65; Cruden; The War that Never Ended, p. 139.

[69]Edward Wakin, Black Fighting Men in United States History (New York: Lothrop, Lee & Shepard Co., 1971), pp. 45-46; Quarles, Douglass, pp. 204-208; McPherson, Negro's Civil War, pp. 166-72.

[70]Official Records, Series 3, Vol. V, pp. 660-62; McPherson, Struggle for Equality, p. 207.

[71]Official Records, Series 3, Vol. V, p. 661; Frederick M. Binder, "Pennsylvania Negro Regiments in the Civil War," Journal of Negro History 37 (October 1952): 383-417.

[72]Quarles, Douglass, pp. 203-209; Huggins, Slave and Citizen, p. 87.

[73]Williams, Negro Troops in the War of the Rebellion, pp. 115-16.

[74]Leslie H. Fishel, Jr., and Benjamin Quarles, eds., The Negro American: A Documentary History (New York: William Morrow & Co., Inc., 1967), p. 232; McPherson, Negro's Civil War, p. 181

CHAPTER II

[1]The War of the Rebellion: Official Records of the Union and Confederate Armies, 128 vols. (Washington: Government Printing Office, 1880-1902), Series 3, Vol. V, p. 661.

[2]John Hope Franklin, From Slavery to Freedom: A History of Negro Americans (New York: Random House, 1969), pp. 290-94; Leon F. Litwack, Been in the Storm So Long: The Aftermath of Slavery (New York: Alfred A. Knopf, Inc., 1979), pp. 79-87.

[3]Dudley T. Cornish, The Sable Arm: Negro Troops in the Union Army, 1861-1865 (New York: W. W. Norton & Co., 1966), p. 188; Franklin, From Slavery to Freedom, p. 291.

[4]James M. McPherson, The Negro's Civil War: How American Negroes Felt and Acted During the War for the Union (New York: Random House, 1965), p. 199.

[5]Cornish, The Sable Arm, pp. 184-85.

[6]Official Records, Series 3, Vol. II, p. 411; Vol. III, p. 1102.

[7]Thomas W. Higginson, Army Life in a Black Regiment (Williamstown, Mass.: Corner House Publishers, 1870; reprinted 1971), pp. 281-84.

[8]Ibid., p. 280; McPherson, Negro's Civil War, pp. 199-203; Franklin, From Slavery to Freedom, p. 291.

[9]Official Records, Series 3, Vol. IV, p. 565.

[10]Ibid., Series 1, Vol. XIV, p. 599.

[11]Cornish, The Sable Arm, pp. 159-60.

[12]Official Records, Series 2, Vol. V, p. 797.

[13]Ibid., pp. 807-808.

[14]Ibid., pp. 940-41; Series 1, Vol. XXIV, Pt. 3, p. 4441

[15]Cornish, The Sable Arm, pp. 161-63.

[16]Official Records, Series 2, Vol. V, p. 712.

[17]Cornish, The Sable Arm, pp. 163-66.

[18]Official Records, Series 2, Vol. VI, p. 163.

[19]Cornish, The Sable Arm, pp. 169-70.

[20]Ibid., pp. 171-72.

[21]Ibid., pp. 173-75; McPherson, Negro's Civil War, pp. 216-17.

[22]George W. Williams, A History of the Negro Troops in the War of the Rebellion, 1861-65 (New York: Harper & Brothers, 1888; reprint ed., New York: Negro Universities Press, 1969), pp. 259-60.

[23]Official Records, Series 1, Vol. XXXII, Pt. 1, p. 588; Cornish, The Sable Arm, p. 177; McPherson, Negro's Civil War, pp. 221-22.

[24]Cornish, The Sable Arm, pp. 175-76.

[25]Peter M. Bergman, The Chronological History of the Negro in America (New York: Harper & Row, Publishers, 1969), pp. 236-40; Franklin, From Slavery to Freedom, p. 291.

[26]Benjamin Quarles, The Negro in the Civil War (Boston: Little, Brown & Co., 1969), pp. 204-205; William L. Katz, Eyewitness: The Negro in American History (New York: Pitman Publishing Corporation, 1971), p. 213.

[27]Katz, Eyewitness, p. 213.

[28]Robert Cruden, The War that Never Ended: The American Civil War (Englewood Cliffs, New Jersey: Prentice-Hall, Inc., 1973); p. 213; McPherson, The Negro's Civil War, pp. 70-71; Adrian Cook, The Armies of the Streets: The New York City Draft Riots of 1863 (Lexington: The University Press of Kentucky, 1974), pp. 77-95; Williston H. Lofton, "Northern Labor and the Negro During the Civil War," Journal of Negro History, 34 (July 1949): 251-73.

[29]Katz, Eyewitness, pp. 213-14.

[30]Joseph T. Wilson, The Black Phalanx: A History of the Negro Soldiers of the United States in the Wars of 1775-1812, 1861-65 (Hartford: American Publishing Co., 1890; reprint ed., New York: Arno Press, 1968), p. 199; Cornish, The Sable Arm pp. 142-44; Williams, Negro Troops in the War of the Rebellion, pp. 215-19.

[31]Official Records, Series 1, Vol. XXVI, Pt. 1, p. 45.

[32]Ibid., Vol. XXIV, Pt. 1, pp. 95-96; Pt. 2, pp. 447-48, 467.

[33]Ibid., Series 3, Vol. III, pp. 452-53.

[34]Williams, Negro Troops in the War of the Rebellion, p. 228.

[35]Official Records, Series 1, Vol. XXII, Pt. 1, pp. 379-81, 449-50.

[36]Williams, Negro Troops in the War of the Rebellion, p. 192.

[37]James T. Robertson, Jr., "Negro Soldiers in the Civil War," Annual Editions, Readings in American History, ed. Terry Chase (Guilford, Conn.: The Dushkin Publishing Group, Inc., 1972-73), pp. 146-56; Official Records, Series 1, Vol. XXVIII, Pt. 1, pp. 15-16.

[38]Williams, Negro Troops in the War of the Rebellion, p. 199.

[39]Official Records, Series 3, Vol. III, p. 696.

[40]Bobby L. Lovett, "The West Tennessee Colored Troops in Civil War Combat," West Tennessee Historical Society Papers 34 (October 1980): 53-70.

[41]Ibid., pp. 54-55.

[42]Official Records, Series 1, Vol. XXI, Pt. 1, pp. 577, 583-85.

[43]Ibid., Series 3, Vol. III, p. 1132.

[44]Cornish, The Sable Arm, p. 251.

[45]Wilson, The Black Phalanx, pp. 166-80; Cornish, The Sable Arm, p. 208.

[46]Cornish, The Sable Arm, pp. 208-209.

[47]Ibid., p. 213.

[48]Official Records, Series 3, Vol. IV, p. 207; Cornish, The Sable Arm, p. 218.

[49]Cornish, The Sable Arm, pp. 222-25.

[50]See Appendix A for list of battles.

[51]Mark Mayo Boatner III, The Civil War Dictionary (New York: David McKay Co., 1959), p. 608; E. B. Long, The Civil War Day by Day: An Almanac 1861-1865 (New York: Doubleday & Co., Inc., 1971), p. 466; Official Records, Series 1, Vol. XXXV, Pt. 1, pp. 298, 315, 341.

[52]Official Records, Series 1, Vol. XXXV, Pt. 1, pp. 298, 315, 341.

[53]Bergman, Chronological History of the Negro, p. 237; McPherson, Negro's Civil War, p. 223; Williams, Negro Troops in the War of the Rebellion, p. 231

[54]Williams, Negro Troops in the War of the Rebellion, pp. 235-37; Benjamin Quarles, The Negro in the Civil War (Boston: Little, Brown & Co., 1969), pp. 297-99.

[55]Official Records, Series 1, Vol. XL, Pt. 1, pp. 705-706; Quarles, Negro in the Civil War, p. 300.

[56]James G. Randall and David Donald, The Civil War and Reconstruction (Boston: D. C. Heath & Co., 1966), pp. 423-24; Quarles, Negro in the Civil War, p. 300.

[57]Boatner, Civil War Dictionary, pp. 647-48; Long, Civil War Day by Day, p. 548.

[58]Wilson, The Black Phalanx, p. 411

[59]Williams, Negro Troops in the War of the Rebellion, pp. 245-46.

[60]Cornish, The Sable Arm, p. 275; Quarles, Negro in the Civil War, p. 301.

[61]Boatner, Civil War Dictionary, p. 648; Cornish, The Sable Arm, p. 275.

[62]Official Records, Series 1, Vol. XL, Pt. 1, pp. 246-48; Boatner, Civil War Dictionary, p. 649.

[63]Official Records, Series 1, Vol. XL, Pt. 1, pp. 118-19; Cornish, The Sable Arm, pp. 276-77.

[64]Official Records, Series 1, Vol. XLII, Pt. 1, pp. 120, 678.

[65]Ibid., pp. 106, 108, 133-34, 136-37; Williams, Negro Troops in the War of the Rebellion, pp. 252-53.

[66]Official Records, Series 1, Vol. XLII, Pt. 1, pp. 848-50; Series 3, Vol. IV, p. 789; Cornish, The Sable Arm, p. 281.

[67]Williams, Negro Troops in the War of the Rebellion, p. 276.

[68]Williams, Negro Troops in the War of the Rebellion, p. 276.

[69]Ibid., p. 277; Wilson, The Black Phalanx, pp. 298-99.

[70]Official Records, Series 1, Vol. XLV, Pt. 1, p. 508; Quarles, Negro in the Civil War, pp. 306-11.

[71]Cornish, The Sable Arm, pp. 265-66.

[72]Williams, Negro Troops in the War of the Rebellion, pp. 291-93.

[73]Ibid., p. 291.

[74]Ibid., pp. 291-93; Official Records, Series 4, Vol. III, pp. 1012-13; Series 1, Vol. XLVI, Pt. 3, pp. 1356-57.

[75]Randall and Donald, Civil War and Reconstruction, pp. 523-24.

[76]Ibid., p. 523; Cornish, The Sable Arm, p. 282; Quarles, Negro in the Civil War, pp. 326-27.

[77]Quarles, Negro in the Civil War, pp. 316-19.

[78]Wilson, The Black Phalanx, pp. 445-46; Randall and Donald, Civil War and Reconstruction, p. 525.

[79]Cornish, The Sable Arm, p. 282; Quarles, Negro in the Civil War, p. 332.

[80]Frederick H. Dyer, A Compendium of the War of the Rebellion, 2 vols. (Dayton, Ohio: Morningside Bookshop, 1908), 2:1720-40.

[81]Official Records, Series 3, Vol. V, p. 661; McPherson, Negro's Civil War, p. 237.

[82]Quarles, Negro in the Civil War, pp. 229-32. For a complete list of all black servicemen awarded the Congressional Medal of Honor, see Appendix B.

CHAPTER III

[1]Herbert Aptheker, "The Negro in the Union Navy," Journal of Negro History 32 (April 1947): 169-70.

[2]Official Records of the Union and Confederate Navies in the War of the Rebellion, 30 vols. (Washington: Government Printing Office, 1897), Series 1, Vol. VI, pp. 0-10.

[3]Ibid., pp. 81, 85-86, 95, 107, 113-14, 252.

[4]Aptheker, "Negro in the Union Navy," p. 176.

[5]Benjamin Quarles, The Negro in the Civil War (Boston: Little, Brown & Co., 1969), p. 229; Official Records Navies, Series 2, Vol. I, pp. 15-23; Aptheker, "Negro in the Union Navy," pp. 177-78.

[6]Official Records Navies, Series 1, Vol. VII, p. 632; XIV, p. 401; XXIV, p. 545; XIII, p. 209.

[7]Ibid., Vol. XXIII, p. 619; XXV, pp. 327-38; XI, pp. 90-91; XII, p. 338; XIX, p. 599; XIV, p. 251.

[8]Aptheker, "Negro in the Union Navy," p. 181.

[9]Official Records Navies, Series 1, Vol. XXIII, p. 639; XXIV, pp. 308-309; Quarles, Negro in the Civil War, pp. 230-31.

[10]Official Records Navies, Series 1, Vol. XII, p. 353; XIII, pp. 257-58.

[11]Ibid., II, pp. 516-17; XV, p. 410; VI, pp. 113-14; XXV, pp. 452-56.

[12]Ibid., XIII, pp. 430-33.

[13]Robert E. Greene, Black Defenders of America: 1775-1793 (Chicago: Johnson Publishing Co., Inc., 1974), p. 90.

[14]Official Records Navies, Series 1, Vol. XII, pp. 821-25; Quarles, Negro in the Civil War, pp. 71-74; James M. McPherson, The Negro's Civil War: How American Negroes Felt and Acted During the War for the Union (New York: Random House, 1965), pp. 154-57.

[15]Quarles, Negro in the Civil War, pp. 91-93; McPherson, Negro's Civil War, pp. 154-58.

[16]Quarles, Negro in the Civil War, p. 93; Greene, Black Defenders, p. 91

[17]McPherson, Negro's Civil War, pp. 153-54; Quarles, Negro in the Civil War, pp. 32-33.

[18]Quarles, Negro in the Civil War, pp. 33-34.

[19]Ibid., pp. 34-35.

[20]Allen Foster, "The Woman Who Saved the Union Navy," Ebony, December 1977, pp. 131-32.

[21]Ibid., pp. 132-35.

[22]Quarles, Negro in the Civil War, p. 232.

[23]Official Records Navies, Series 1, Vol. XV, pp. 191, 197.

[24]Ibid., XVIII, p. 179; XXI, p. 437.

[25]Ibid., III, pp. 67-68.

CHAPTER IV

[1]Allan Pinkerton, The Spy of the Rebellion: A True History of the Spy System of the United States Army During the Late Rebellion (Kansas City: Kansas City Publishing Co., pp. 343-44; William L. Katz, Eyewitness: The Negro in American History (New York: Pitman Publishing Corporation, 1971), p. 209.

[2]Pinkerton, The Spy of the Rebellion, pp. 344-57.

[3]Ibid., pp. 358-93; Harnett T. Kane, Spies for the Blue and Gray (New York: Hanover House, 1954), pp. 97-101; Allen Foster, "John Scobell: Union Spy in the Civil War," Ebony, October 1978, pp. 73-81.

[4]Benjamin Quarles, The Negro in the Civil War (Boston: Little, Brown & Co., 1969), pp. 78-87.

[5]Kane, Spies for the Blue and Gray, pp. 231-39. (For a more detailed discussion of Mrs. Elizabeth Van Lew's activities, see Chapter 11).

[6]Quarles, The Negro in the Civil War, pp. 80-81.

[7]The War of the Rebellion: Official Records of the Union and Confederate Armies, 128 vols. (Washington: Government Printing Office, 1880-1902), Series 1, Vol. X, Pt. 2, p. 162.

[8]Sarah Bradford, Harriet Tubman: The Moses of Her People (Secaucus, New Jersey: The Citadel Press, 1974), pp. 138-42; Judith Nies, Seven Women: Portraits from the American Radical Tradition (New York: Penguin Books, 1979), pp. 35-43; James Loewenberg and Ruth Bogin, eds., Black Women in Nineteenth-Century American Life: Their Words, Their Thoughts, Their Feelings (Philadelphia: The Pennsylvania State University Press, 1976), pp. 219-21.

[9]Gerda Lerner, ed., Black Women in White America: A Documentary History (New York: Random House, 1972), pp. 63-65, 326-29; Nies, Seven Women, pp. 52-56; Bradford, Harriet Tubman, pp. 136-37.

[10]Quarles, The Negro in the Civil War, pp. 81-82.

[11]Kane, Spies for the Blue and Gray, pp. 11-16; Official Records, Series 2, Vol. IV, pp. 150, 894-97; Vol. V, pp. 98, 103, 148, 216, 322, 373, 480, 522; Vol. VI, pp. 13, 18, 26, 29, 141; Series 3, Vol. I, p. 367.

[12]Official Records, Series 1, Vol. XVIII, p. 675; Vol. XXII, pp. 724-25; Series 3, Vol. IV, pp. 893-94.

[13]Bobby L. Lovett, "The Negro in Tennessee, 1861-1866: A Socio-Military History of the Civil War Era" (Ph.D. dissertation, University of Arkansas, 1978), pp. 29-37.

[14]Wyatt Blassingame, William Tecumseh Sherman: Defender of the Union (Englewood Cliffs, New Jersey: Prentice-Hall, Inc., 1970), pp. 120-31; Miles Lane, ed., "War is Hell!": William T. Sherman's Personal Narrative of His March Through Georgia (Savannah: The Beehive Press, 1974), pp. 144-79; Quarles, Negro in the Civil War, pp. 318-21.

[15]James M. McPherson, The Negro's Civil War: How American Negroes Felt and Acted During the War for the Union (New York: Random House, 1965), pp. 150-51; John McElroy, Andersonville: A Story of Rebel Military Persons (Toledo: D. R. Locke, 1879), pp. 134-37; Ovid L. Futch, History of Andersonville Prison (Indiantown, Florida: University of Florida Press, 1968), p. 51.

[16]Dorothy Clarke Wilson, Lone Woman: The Story of Elizabeth Blackwell, The First Woman Doctor (Boston: Little, Brown & Co., 1970), pp. 383-91; Sylvia G. Dannet, Noble Women of the North (New York: Thomas Yoseloff, 1959), pp. 53-57.

[17]Dannet, Noble Women of the North, pp. 57-62; Wilson Lone Woman, pp. 385-91; Aloysius Plaisance and Leo F. Schelver, III, "Federal Military Hospitals in Nashville, May and June, 1863," Tennessee Historical Quarterly 29 (1970): 166-75.

[18]Nies, Seven Women, pp. 52-54; Lerner, Black Women in White America, pp. 326-29; Loewenberg and Bogin, Black Women in Nineteenth-Century, pp. 219-21.

[19]Leslie H. Fishel, Jr., and Benjamin Quarles, eds., The Negro American: A Documentary History (New York: William Morrow & Co., Inc., 1967), pp. 236-37; Loewenberg and Bogin, Black Women in Nineteenth-Century, pp. 89-94, 234-42; Lerner, Black Women in White America, pp. 99, 240-43.

[20]Lerner, Black Women in White America, pp. 370-75.

[21]John Vincent Cimprich, Jr., "Slavery Amidst Civil War in Tennessee: The Death of an Institution" (Ph.D. dissertation, Ohio State University, 1977), pp. 97-119; Lovett, "The Negro in Tennessee, 1861-1866," pp. 25-26.

[22]McPherson, Negro's Civil War, p. 139; John Hope Franklin, From Slavery to Freedom: A History of Negro Americans (New York: Random House, 1969), pp. 275-77.

[23]Sister Elizabeth A. Allen, "Women Missionaries and the Education of the Blacks in Hampton, Virginia, 1861-1868" (Master's thesis, Middle Tennessee State University, 1977), pp. 6-9.

[24]Ibid., pp. 20-24; Franklin, From Slavery to Freedom, pp. 275-77.

[25]Official Records, Series 1, Vol. VI, p. 218; Louis S. Gerteis, From Contraband to Freedman: Federal Policy Toward Southern Blacks (Westport, Conn.: Greenwood Press, Inc., 1973), pp. 49-55.

[26]Dudley T. Cornish, "The Union Army as a School for Negroes," Journal of Negro History 37 (May 1952): 368-82; Elizabeth Ware Pearson, ed., Letters From Port Royal 1862-1868 (New York: Arno Press & New York Times, 1969), pp. 15-35; Willie Lee Rose, Rehearsal for Reconstruction: The Port Royal Experiment (New York: Random House, Inc., 1964), p. 203.

[27]Ray Allen Billington, ed., The Journal of Charlotte Forten: A Free Negro in the Slave Era (New York: The Macmillan Co., 1967), pp. 7-26.

[28]Ibid., pp. 27-41; Lerner, Black Women in White America, pp. 94-99; Rose, Rehearsal for Reconstruction, pp. 161-62; Loewenberg and Bogin, Black Women in Nineteenth-Century, pp. 283-85; Edward T. James, et al., eds. Notable American Women, 1607-1950: A Biographical Dictionary, 4 vols. (Cambridge, Mass.: Harvard University Press, 1971), 2:95-97.

[29]McPherson, Negro's Civil War, pp. 133-39.

[30]Elizabeth Jacoway, Yankee Missionaries in the South: The Penn School Experiment (Baton Rouge: Louisiana State University Press, 1980), pp. 25-32; Merton L. Dillon, The Abolitionists: The Growth of a Dissenting Minority (New York: W. W. Norton & Co., 1979), pp. 262-63.

[31]Lerner, Black Women in White America, pp. 27-29, 99-101; Fishel and Quarles, The Negro American, pp. 236-37; George R. Bentley, A History of the Freedmen's Bureau (New York: Octagon Books, 1974), p. 170; Loewenberg and Bogin, Black Women in Nineteenth-Century, pp. 89-94.

[32]John W. Blassingame, "The Union Army as an Educational Institution for Negroes, 1862–1865," Journal of Negro Education 34 (1965): 152–53; Cornish, "Union Army as a School for Negroes," pp. 374–82; Ellis O. Knox, "The Origin and Development of the Negro Separate School," Journal of Negro Education 16 (1947): 273–75.

[33]Blassingame, "The Union Army as an Educational Institution for Negroes," pp. 153–54; Official Records, Series 3, Vol. III, pp. 1139–44; McPherson, Negro's Civil War, pp. 133–39.

[34]Howard A. White, The Freedmen's Bureau in Louisiana (Baton Rouge: Louisiana State University Press, 1970), pp. 166–68; Blassingame, "The Union Army as an Educational Institution for Negroes," pp. 153–54.

[35]White, The Freedmen's Bureau in Louisiana, p. 167.

[36]Thomas W. Higginson, Army Life in a Black Regiment (Williamstown, Mass.: Corner House Publishers, 1870; reprinted 1971), p. 254; Cornish, "Union Army as a School for Negroes," pp. 374–82; Blassingame, "The Union Army as an Educational Institution for Negroes," pp. 154–55.

[37]Blassingame, "The Union Army as an Educational Institution for Negroes," p. 156; W. Augustus Low and Virgil A. Clift, Encyclopedia of Black America (New York: McGraw-Hill, Inc., 1981), pp. 820–21.

[38]Official Records, Series 1, Vol. XLII, Pt. 1, pp. 848–50; Series 3, Vol. IV, p. 789; Dudley T. Cornish, The Sable Arm: Negro Troops in the Union Army, 1861–1865 (New York: W. W. Norton & Co., 1966), p. 281.

[39]Bentley, A History of the Freedmen's Bureau, p. 21.

[40]McPherson, Negro's Civil War, pp. 133–38; Franklin, From Slavery to Freedom, p. 275.

[41]Elizabeth Keckley, Behind the Scenes: Thirty Years a Slave and Four Years in the White House (New York: G. W. Carleton & Co., 1868, reprint ed., New York: Arno Press & The New York Times, 1968), pp. 17–85.

[42]Ibid., pp. 112–16; Loewenberg and Bogin, Black Women in Nineteenth-Century, pp. 70–77.

[43]James McPherson, The Struggle for Equality: Abolitionists and the Negro in the Civil War and Reconstruction (Princeton: Princeton University Press, 1968), p. 178; Gerteis, From Contraband to Freedman, pp. 135-39; Bentley, A History of the Freedmen's Bureau, pp. 21-24.

[44]John G. Sproat, "Blueprint for Radical Reconstruction," Journal of Southern History 23 (February 1957): 28-29; Rose, Rehearsal for Reconstruction, pp. 144-52.

[45]Official Records, Series 3, Vol. III, pp. 73-74; Sproat, "Blueprint for Radical Reconstruction," pp. 29-34.

[46]Official Records, Series 3, Vol. III, pp. 430-54; Vol. IV, pp. 381-82.

[47]Sproat, "Blueprint for Radical Reconstruction," pp. 34-35; Bentley, A History of the Freedmen's Bureau, pp. 25-29; Official Records, Series 3, Vol. IV, pp. 289-382.

[48]McPherson, Struggle for Equality, pp. 186-91; Bentley, A History of the Freedmen's Bureau, pp. 40-49.

[49]Bentley, A History of the Freedmen's Bureau, pp. 49-52.

[50]For a discussion of white and black reactions to the Freedmen's Bureau, see Paul D. Phillips, "White Reaction to the Freedmen's Bureau in Tennessee," Tennessee Historical Quarterly 25 (1966): 50-62; Lovett, "The Negro in Tennessee, 1861-1866," pp. 175-91.

[51]W. E. B. DuBois, "Reconstruction and Its Benefits," American Historical Review 15 (July 1910): 781-99; Franklin, From Slavery to Freedom, pp. 306-309; Weymouth T. Jordan, "The Freedmen's Bureau of Tennessee," East Tennessee Historical Society Papers 11 (1939): 47-61; Preston R. Merry, "The Freedmen's Bureau in Tennessee, 1865-1869" (Master's thesis, Fisk University, 1938).

[52]Leon F. Litwack, North of Slavery: The Negro in the Free States, 1790-1860 (Chicago: The University of Chicago Press, 1961), pp. 15-16; Guion Griffis Johnson, "Southern Paternalism Toward Negroes After Emancipation," Journal of Southern History 23 (November 1957): 484-85.

[53]McPherson, Negro's Civil War, pp. 245-46; Litwack, North of Slavery, pp. 113-17.

[54]Leon F. Litwack, Been in the Storm So Long: The Aftermath of Slavery (New York: Alfred A. Knopf, 1979), pp. 77-82; Benjamin Quarles, Frederick Douglass (New York: Atheneum, 1969), pp. 187-88.

[55]Benjamin Quarles, Great Lives Observed: Frederick Douglass (Englewood Cliffs, N.J.: Prentice-Hall, 1968); p. 11; Nathan Irvin Huggins, Slave and Citizen: The Life of Frederick Douglass (Boston: Little, Brown & Co., 1980), p. 101.

[56]Wendell Phillips, Speeches, Lectures, and Letters (New York: Lee & Shepard, 1884; reprint ed., New York: Negro Universities Press, 1968), pp. 2-10.

[57]Ibid., pp. 419-34.

[58]McPherson, Struggle for Equality, pp. 234-37.

[59]McPherson, Negro's Civil War, pp. 249-54; Litwack, North of Slavery, pp. 70-74.

[60]Herbert Aptheker, ed., A Documentary History of the Negro People in the United States (New York: The Citadel Press, 1968), pp. 502-506.

[61]McPherson, Negro's Civil War, pp. 265-70; Litwack, North of Slavery, pp. 113-17.

[62]John W. Blassingame, Black New Orleans, 1860-1880 (Chicago: The University of Chicago Press, 1973), pp. 173-90.

[63]Roy P. Blaser, ed., The Collected Works of Abraham Lincoln, 9 vols. (New Brunswick, New Jersey, 1953), 3:53-56; McPherson, Struggle for Equality, pp. 240-41

[64]Huggins, Slave and Citizen, pp. 95-97; Richard H. Sewell, Ballots for Freedom: Antislavery Politics in the United States, 1837-1860 (New York: W. W. Norton & Co., 1980), pp. 321-23; George M. Fredrickson, "A Man But Not a Brother: Abraham Lincoln and Racial Equality," Journal of Southern History 41 (February 1975): 39-58.

[65]McPherson, Struggle for Equality, pp. 242-48.

[66]Rose, Rehearsal for Reconstruction, pp. 214-15; McPherson, Negro's Civil War, pp. 296-97.

[67]Gerteis, From Contraband to Freedmen, pp. 57-58; Lloyd Lewis, Sherman: Fighting Prophet (New York: Harcourt, Brace & Co., 1932), pp. 480-82; James M. Merrill, William Tecumseh Sherman (New York: Rand McNally & Co., 1971), pp. 277-79.

146

[68]Benjamin P. Thomas and Harold M. Hayman, <u>Stanton: The Life and Times of Lincoln's Secretary of War</u> (New York: Alfred A. Knopf, 1962), pp. 343-46; Merrill, <u>William T. Sherman</u>, p. 482.

[69]Rose, <u>Rehearsal for Reconstruction</u>, pp. 327-31; Quarles, <u>The Negro in the Civil War</u>, pp. 322-24; McPherson, <u>Negro's Civil War</u>, pp. 299-300; Lewis, <u>Sherman</u>, p. 482.

[70]McPherson, <u>Struggle for Equality</u>, p. 258.

[71]Gerteis, <u>From Contraband to Freedmen</u>, pp. 57-58; 150-51; McPherson, <u>Struggle for Equality</u>, p. 258.

[72]McPherson, <u>Negro's Civil War</u>, p. 300; Rose, <u>Rehearsal for Reconstruction</u>, pp. 346-77; Corinne K. Hoexter, <u>Black Crusader: Frederick Douglass</u> (Chicago: Rand McNally & Co., 1970), pp. 201-206; Huggins, <u>Slave and Citizen</u>, p. 117.

[73]Quarles, <u>Negro in the Civil War</u>, pp. 282-84; for a full discussion of the lessee system, see Chapter 9 in Gerteis, <u>From Contraband to Freedmen</u>, pp. 153-67.

[74]Janet Sharp Hermann, <u>The Pursuit of a Dream</u> (New York: Oxford University Press, 1981), pp. 3-9.

[75]Ibid., for a detailed discussion of Davis's brick mansion, the landscaping, and buildings on the plantation, see pages 9-11.

[76]Ibid., pp. 11-34.

[77]Gerteis, <u>From Contraband to Freedmen</u>, pp. 175-81; Quarles, <u>The Negro in the Civil War</u>, pp. 285-86.

[78]Lovett, "The Negro in Tennessee, 1861-1866," pp. 154-60; Thomas J. Ladenburg and Williams S. McFeely, <u>The Black Man in the Land of Equality</u> (New York: Hayden Book Co., Inc., 1969), pp. 15-20; Quarles, <u>The Negro in the Civil War</u>, pp. 288-90. For an excellent study of the black family in New Orleans during the Civil War, see Chapter 4 in Blassingame, <u>Black New Orleans</u>, 1860-1880, pp. 79-105.

[79]Quarles, <u>The Negro in the Civil War</u>, pp. 287-88; Lovett, "The Negro in Tennessee, 1861-1866," pp. 157-60.

[80]Blassingame, <u>Black New Orleans</u>, 1860-1880, pp. 148-49.

[81]Ibid., pp. 148-52; Lovett, "The Negro in Tennessee, 1861-1866," pp. 160-65. For an excellent discussion of black spirituals in Colonel Thomas Higginson's black regiment, see Chapter 10 in Higginson, <u>Army Life in a Black Regiment</u>, pp. 197-222.

[82]Huggins, <u>Slave and Citizen</u>, pp. 100-102; McPherson, Negro's Civil War, pp. 301-306.

[83]McPherson, Negro's Civil War, pp. 307-308; Huggins, Slave and Citizen, pp. 102-103.

CHAPTER V

[1]See Appendix C for black soldiers accredited to each state during the Civil War.

[2]Thomas W. Higginson, Army Life in a Black Regiment (Williamstown, Mass.: Corner House Publishers, 1870; reprinted 1971), p. 267.

BIBLIOGRAPHY

PRIMARY SOURCES

A. Official Records

Official Records of the Union and Confederate Navies in the War of the Rebellion. 30 vols. Washington: Government Printing Office, 1894-1922.

The War of the Rebellion: Official Records of the Union and Confederate Armies. 128 vols. Washington: Government Printing Office, 1880-1902.

B. Edited Works

Aptheker, Herbert, ed. A Documentary History of the Negro People in the United States. 2 vols. New York: The Citadel Press, 1968.

Basler, Roy P., ed. The Collected Works of Abraham Lincoln. 9 vols. New Brunswick, New Jersey, 1953.

Billington, Roy Allen, ed. The Journal of Charlotte Forten: A Free Negro in the Slave Era. New York: The Macmillan Co., 1967.

Fishel, Leslie H., Jr., and Quarles, Benjamin, eds. The Negro American: A Documentary History. New York: William Morrow & Co., Inc., 1967.

Foner, Philip S., ed. The Life and Writings of Frederick Douglass: The Civil War 1861-1865. 4 vols. New York: International Publishers, 1952.

Lerner, Gerda, ed. Black Women in White America: A Documentary History. New York: Random House, 1972.

Loewenberg, James, and Bogin, Ruth, eds. Black Women in Nineteenth-Century American Life: Their Words, Their Thoughts, Their Feelings. Philadelphia: The Pennsylvania State University Press, 1976.

149

Mills, Lane, ed. "War is Hell": William T. Wherman's Personal
Narrative of His March Through Georgia. Savannah: The
Beehive Press, 1974.

Pearson, Elizabeth Ware, ed. Letters from Port Royal 1862-1868.
New York: Arno Press & New York Times, 1969.

C. Books

Higginson, Thomas W. Army Life in a Black Regiment.
Williamstown, Mass.: Corner House Publishers, 1870;
reprint ed., 1971.

Keckley, Elizabeth. Behind the Scenes: Thirty Years A Slave and
Four Years in the White House. New York: G. W. Carleton
& Co., 1868; reprint ed., New York: Arno Press & The New
York Times, 1968.

Phillips, Wendell. Speeches, Lectures, and Letters. New York:
Lee & Shepard, 1884; reprint ed., New York: Negro
Universities Press, 1968.

Pinkerton, Allan. The Spy of the Rebellion: A True History of
the Spy System of the United States Army During the Late
Rebellion. Kansas City: Kansas City Publishing Co., 1883.

SECONDARY SOURCES

A. Reference Works

Boatner, Mark Mayo III. The Civil War Dictionary. New York:
David McKay Co., 1959.

Dyer, Frederick H. A Compendium of the War of the Rebellion.
2 vols. Dayton, Ohio: Morningside Bookshop, 1908.

James, Edward T., James, Janet Wilson, and Boyer, Paul S.,
eds. Notable American Women, 1607-1950: A Biographical
Dictionary. 4 vols. Cambridge, Mass.: Harvard University
Press, 1971.

Kaiser, Ernest, and Ploski, Harry A. The Negro Almanac. New
York: The Bellwether Co., 1971.

Long, E. B. The Civil War Day by Day: An Almanac 1861-1865. New York: Doubleday & Co., Inc., 1971.

Low, W. Augustus, and Clift, Virgil A. Encyclopedia of Black America. New York: McGraw-Hill, Inc., 1981.

B. Books

Bentley, George R. A History of the Freedmen's Bureau. New York: Octagon Books, 1974.

Bergman, Peter M. The Chronological History of the Negro in America. New York: Harper & Row, Publishers, 1969.

Blassingame, John W. Black New Orleans 1860-1880. Chicago: The University of Chicago Press, 1973.

Blassingame, Wyatt. William Tecumseh Sherman: Defender of the Union. Englewood Cliffs, New Jersey: Prentice-Hall, Inc., 1970.

Bradford, Sarah. Harriet Tubman: The Moses of Her People. Secaucus, New Jersey: The Citadel Press, 1974.

Brewer, James H. The Confederate Negro: Virginia's Craftsmen and Military Laborers 1861-1865. Durham, N.C.: Duke University Press, 1969.

Cook, Adrian. The Armies of the Streets: The New York City Draft Riots of 1863. Lexington: The University Press of Kentucky, 1974.

Cornish, Dudley T. The Sable Arm: Negro Troops in the Union Army, 1861-1865. New York: W. W. Norton & Co., 1966.

Cruden, Robert. The War that Never Ended: The American Civil War. Englewood Cliffs, New Jersey: Prentice-Hall, Inc., 1973.

Dannet, Sylvia. Noble Women of the North. New York: Thomas Yoseloff, 1959.

Dillon, Merton L. The Abolitionists: The Growth of a Dissenting Minority. New York: W. W. Norton & Co., 1979.

Egan, Ferol. Fremont: Explorer for a Restless Nation. New York: Doubleday & Co., Inc., 1977.

Franklin, John Hope. From Slavery to Freedom: A History of Negro Americans. New York· Random House, 1969.

_____. The Emancipation Proclamation. Garden City, New York: Doubleday & Co., Inc., 1965.

Futch, Ovid L. History of Andersonville Prison. Indiantown, Florida: University of Florida Press, 1968.

Gerteis, Louis S. From Contraband to Freedmen· Federal Policy Toward Southern Blacks. Westport, Conn.: Greenwood Press, Inc., 1973.

Graham, Shirley. There Was Once a Slave: The Heroic Story of Frederick Douglass. New York: Julian Messner, Inc., 1947.

Greene, Robert E. Black Defenders of America: 1775-1973. Chicago: Johnson Publishing Co., Inc., 1974.

Gutman, Herbert C. The Black Family in Slavery and Freedom, 1750-1925. New York: Vintage Books, 1976.

Hermann, Janet Sharp. The Pursuit of a Dream. New York: Oxford University Press, 1981.

Hoexter, Corinne K. Black Crusader: Frederick Douglass. Chicago: Rand McNally & Co., 1970.

Huggins, Nathan Irvin. Slave and Citizen: The Life of Frederick Douglass. Boston: Little, Brown & Co., 1980.

Jacoway, Elizabeth. Yankee Missionaries in the South· The Penn School Experiment. Baton Rouge: Louisiana State University Press, 1980.

Kane, Harnett T. Spies for the Blue and Gray. New York: Hanover House, 1954.

Katz, William L. Eyewitness: The Negro in American History. New York: Pitman Publishing Corporation, 1971.

Ladenburg, Thomas J., and McFreely, William S. The Black Man in the Land of Equality. New York: Hayden Book Co., Inc., 1969.

Lewis, Lloyd. Sherman: Fighting Prophet. New York: Harcourt, Brace & Co., 1932.

Litwack, Leon F. Been in the Storm So Long: The Aftermath of Slavery. New York: Alfred A. Knopf, Inc., 1979.

_____. North of Slavery: The Negro in the Free States, 1790-1860.

McElroy, John. Andersonville: A Story of Rebel Military Prisons. Toledo: D. R. Lock, 1879.

McPherson, James M. Ordeal By Fire: The Civil War and Reconstruction. New York: Alfred A. Knopf, 1982.

_____. The Negro's Civil War: How American Negroes Felt and Acted During the War for the Union. New York: Random House, 1965.

_____. The Struggle for Equality: Abolitionists and the Negro in the Civil War and Reconstruction. Princeton: Princeton University Press, 1968.

Merrill, James M. William Tecumseh Sherman. New York: Rand McNally & Co., 1971.

Nies, Judith. Seven Women: Portraits from the American Radical Tradition. New York: Penguin Books, 1979.

Oates, Stephen B. With Malice Toward None: The Life of Abraham Lincoln. New York: Harper & Row, Publishers, 1977.

Quarles, Benjamin. Frederick Douglass. New York: Atheneum, 1969.

_____. Great Lives Observed: Frederick Douglass. Englewood Cliffs, N.J.: Prentice-Hall, 1968.

_____. Lincoln and the Negro. New York· Oxford University Press, 1962.

_____. The Negro in the Civil War. Boston: Little, Brown & Co., 1969.

Randall, James G., and Donald, David. The Civil War and Reconstruction. Boston: D. C. Heath & Co., 1966.

Roark, James L. Masters Without Slaves: Southern Planters in the Civil War and Reconstruction. New York: W. W. Norton & Co., 1977.

Robertson, James T., Jr. "Negro Soldiers in the Civil War," Annual Edutions, Readings in American History. Edited by Terry Chase. Guilford, Conn.: The Dushkin Publishing Group, Inc., 1972-73.

Rose, Willie Lee. Rehearsal for Reconstruction: The Port Royal Experiment. New York: Oxford University Press, 1964.

Sandburg, Carl. Abraham Lincoln: The War Years. 4 vols. New York: Harcourt, Brace & World, Inc., 1939.

Sewell, Richard H. Ballots for Freedom: Antislavery Politics in the United States, 1837-1860. New York: W. W. Norton & Co., 1980.

Thomas, Benjamin P., and Hyman, Harold M. Stanton: The Life and Times of Lincoln's Secretary of War. New York: Alfred A. Knopf, 1962.

Trefousse, Hans L. Ben Butler: The South Called Him Beast. New York: Octagon Books, 1974.

_____. Lincoln's Decision for Emancipation. New York: J. B. Lippincott Co., 1975.

Wakin, Edward. Black Fighting Men in United States History. New York: Lathrop, Lee & Shepard Co., 1971.

White, Howard A. The Freedmen's Bureau in Louisiana. Baton
Rouge: Louisiana State University Press, 1970.

Williams, George W. A History of the Negro Troops in the War
of the Rebellion, 1861-1865. New York: Harper & Brothers,
1888; reprint ed., New York: Negro Universities Press, 1969.

Wilson, Dorothy Clarke. Lone Woman· The Story of Elizabeth
Blackwell, The First Woman Doctor. Boston: Little, Brown
& Co., 1970.

Wilson, Joseph T. The Black Phalanx: A History of the Negro
Soldiers of the United States in the Wars of 1775-1812,
1861-1865. Hartford: American Publishing Co., 1890; reprint
ed., New York: Arno Press, 1968.

C. Theses and Dissertations

Allen, Sister Elizabeth A. "Women Missionaries and the
Education of the Blacks in Hampton, Virginia, 1861-1868."
Master's thesis, Middle Tennessee State University, 1977.

Cimprich, John Vincent, Jr. "Slavery Amidst Civil War in
Tennessee: The Death of an Institution." Ph.D. dissertation,
Ohio State University, 1977.

Lovett, Bobby Lee. "The Negro in Tennessee, 1861-1866: A
Socio-Military History of the Civil War Era." Ph.D.
dissertation, University of Arkansas, 1978.

Merry, Preston R. "The Freedmen's Bureau in Tennessee, 1865-
1869." Master's thesis, Fisk University, 1938.

Stubblefield, Ruth L. "The Education of the Negro in Tennessee
During the Civil War." Master's thesis, Fisk University,
1943.

Van Dyke, Roger Raymond. "The Free Negro in Tennessee, 1790-
1860." Ph.D. dissertation, Florida State University, 1972.

D. Periodical Articles

Aptheker, Herbert. "The Negro in the Union Navy." Journal of Negro History 32 (April 1947) : 169-181.

Binder, Frederick M. "Pennsylvania Negro Regiments in the Civil War." Journal of Negro History 37 (October 1952) : 383-417.

Blassingame, John W. "The Union Army as an Educational Institution for Negroes, 1862-1865." Journal of Negro Education 34 (1965) :152-66.

Brewer, W. M. "Lincoln and the Border States." Journal of Negro History 34 (January 1949) :46-72.

Castel, Albert. "The Fort Pillow Massacre: A Fresh Examination of the Evidence." Civil War History 4 (1958) : 40-48.

Cornish, Dudley T. "The Union Army as a School for Negroes." Journal of Negro History 37 (May 1952) :368-82.

Dyer, Brainerd. "The Treatment of Colored Union Troops by the Confederates, 1861-65." Journal of Negro History 20 (1935): 273-86.

DuBois, W. E. B. "Reconstruction and Its Benefits." American Historical Review 15 (July 1910) :781-99.

Foster, Allen. "John Scobell: Union Spy in the Civil War." Ebony, October 1978, pp. 73-81.

_____. "The Woman Who Saved the Union Navy." Ebony, December 1977, pp. 131-34.

Frederickson, George M. "A Man But Not A Brother: Abraham Lincoln and Racial Equality." Journal of Southern History 41 (February 1975) :39-58.

Imes, William L. "The Legal Status of Free Negroes and Slaves in Tennessee." Journal of Negro History 4 (1919) :254-73.

Johnson, Guion Griffis. "Southern Paternalism Toward Negroes After Emancipation." Journal of Southern History 23 (November 1957) :483-509.

Jordan, Weymouth T. "The Freedmen's Bureau of Tennessee." East Tennessee Historical Society Papers 11 (1939):47-61.

Knox, Ellis O. "The Origin and Development of the Negro Separate School." Journal of Negro Education 16 (1947) : 269-79.

Lofton, Williston H. "Northern Labor and the Negro During the Civil War." Journal of Negro History 34 (July 1949) ·251-73.

Lovett, Bobby I.. "The West Tennessee Colored Troops in Civil War Combat." West Tennessee Society Papers 34 (October 1980) :53-70.

Lowe, W. A. "The Freedmen's Bureau and Civil Rights in Maryland." Journal of Negro History 37 (July 1952) :: 221-47.

Mehlinger, Louis R. "The Attitude of the Free Negro Towards Colonization." Journal of Negro History 1 (1916) :276-301.

Nelson, Bernard H. "Confederate Slave Impressment Legislation, 1861-1865." Journal of Negro History 31 (October 1946) :392-410.

Patton, James W. "The Progress of Emancipation in Tennessee." Journal of Negro History 17 (1932) :76-102.

Phillips, Paul D. "White Reaction to the Freedmen's Bureau in Tennessee." Tennessee Historical Quarterly 25 (1966) :50-62.

Plaisance, Aloysius, and Schelner, Leo F., III. "Federal Military Hospitals in Nashville, May and June, 1863." Tennessee Historical Quarterly 29 (1970) :166-75.

Roberts, S. O. "The Education of Negroes in Tennessee." _Journal of Negro Education_ 16 (1947) :417-24.

Scheips, Paul J. "Lincoln and the Chiriqui Colonization Project." _Journal of Negro History_ 37 (October 1952): 418-53.

Shannon, Fred A. "The Federal Government and the Negro Soldier, 1861-1865." _Journal of Negro History_ 11 (1926) :563-70.

Sproat, John G. "Blueprint for Radical Reconstruction." _Journal of Southern History_ 23 (February 1957) :25-44.

Walker, Cam. "Corinth, the Story of a Contraband Camp." _Civil War History_ 20 (1974) :5-22.

Wesley, Charles H. "The Employment of the Negroes as Soldiers in the Confederate Army." _Journal of Negro History_ 4 (1919) :239-53.

Index

ABOUT THE AUTHOR

Joe H. Mays is Professor of History at Jackson State Community College. Born in Jackson, Tennessee (Madison County), he received his B. A. from Lane College, M. S. from the University of Tennessee at Martin, and D. A. from Middle Tennessee State University in 1982.

Dr. Mays was the recipient of an East-West summer scholarship to the University of Hawaii and a N.D.E.A. history fellowship in 1965, a National Science Foundation sociology fellowship to Southern University in Baton Rouge in 1966, an institutional doctoral grant in 1977, and Middle Tennessee State University awarded him a D. A. grant in 1978.

Before employment at Jackson State Community College in 1968 as its first black instructor, the author was assistant principal, assistant football coach, and teacher of high school history in Dyersburg, Tennessee. He has contributed numerous articles to local publications.